Income Redistribution
from Social Security

Income Redistribution from Social Security

Don Fullerton and
Brent Mast

The AEI Press

Publisher for the American Enterprise Institute
WASHINGTON, D.C.

Available in the United States from the AEI Press, c/o Client Distribution Services, 193 Edwards Drive, Jackson, TN 38301. To order, call toll free: 1-800-343-4499. Distributed outside the United States by arrangement with Eurospan, 3 Henrietta Street, London WC2E 8LU, England.

HD
7105.35
.U6
F85
2005

Library of Congress Cataloging-in-Publication Data
Fullerton, Don
  Income redistribution from social security/ by Don Fullerton and Brent Mast.
  p. cm.
  Includes bibliographical references.
  ISBN 0-8447-4214-7 (pbk. : alk. paper)
  1. Old age pensions—United States. 2. Social security—United States. 3. Income distribution—United States. 4. Distributive justice—United States. I. Mast, Brent D. II. Title.

HD7105.35.U6F85 2005
368.4'3'00973—dc22

2004027563

10 09 08 07 06 05 04   1 2 3 4 5 6 7

© 2005 by the American Enterprise Institute for Public Policy Research, Washington, D.C. All rights reserved. No part of this publication may be used or reproduced in any manner whatsoever without permission in writing from the American Enterprise Institute except in the case of brief quotations embodied in news articles, critical articles, or reviews. The views expressed in the publications of the American Enterprise Institute are those of the authors and do not necessarily reflect the views of the staff, advisory panels, officers, or trustees of AEI.

Printed in the United States of America

Contents

LIST OF ILLUSTRATIONS — vii
ACKNOWLEDGMENTS — ix
1. INTRODUCTION — 1
2. THE SOCIAL SECURITY SYSTEM — 5
   Taxes 5
     Coverage 5
     Tax Rates 5
     Income Subject to Taxation 7
     Tax Incidence 10
     Income Taxes 11
   Benefits 12
     Retirement Age 12
     Eligibility 13
     Benefit Formula 13
     Distribution of Benefits 14
3. DIFFERENCES IN STUDIES THAT MEASURE REDISTRIBUTION — 17
   Data 17
     Aggregate versus Microdata 17
     Data Sets in Micro Simulation Studies 18
   Measures of Redistribution 19
     Income Comparisons 19
     Absolute Redistribution Measures 20
     Relative Redistribution Measures 20
4. SEVEN FACTORS THAT AFFECT REDISTRIBUTION — 22
   Differences in Mortality 22
     Mortality and Socioeconomic Status 22
     Mortality and Social Security Redistribution Studies 28

Income Measures 31
  Aggregate versus Individual Income 31
  Annual versus Lifetime Income 32
  Covered Earnings versus Total Earnings 33
  Own Benefits versus Spouse and Survivor Benefits 34
  Individual versus Family Income 35
  Potential versus Actual Income 35
  Gross versus Net Income 37
  Cost of Living 38
Social Security Taxes 39
  Coverage 39
  Tax Rates 40
  Amount of Income Subject to Taxation 41
Discount Rate 42
Retirement Age 44
  Age of Eligibility 44
  Retirement Trends 44
  Retirement and Socioeconomic Status 47
  Retirement and Social Security Policy 49
  Retirement Ages in Redistribution Studies 50
Cohort Analyzed 51
  Coverage 51
  Net Benefits 53
  Social Security Policy, SES, and Progressivity 54
Behavioral Effects 56
  Earnings 57
  Retirement Age 58
  Savings 59
  Resources Devoted to Obtaining Net Transfers 60
  General Equilibrium Effects 61
  Uncertainty 62

5. CONCLUSIONS 64
NOTES 67
REFERENCES 69
ABOUT THE AUTHORS 75

Illustrations

TABLES
1 Tax Rates as a Percent of Taxable Earnings   8
2 Maximum Income Subject to Social Security
    Taxes, 1937–2002   9
3 Full Retirement Age and Early Retirement Reductions   12
4 Social Security Replacement Rates, 1940–2040   15
5 Average Retirement Age and Expected Retirement, 1950–55
    through 1995–2000   46

FIGURES
1 Percent of Labor Force Covered by Social Security, 1939–99   6
2 Percent of Earnings Covered by Social Security, 1950–99   7
3 Taxable Maximum Wages Relative to Average
    Wages, 1951–2000   10
4 Percent of Workers with Earnings below Taxable Maximum,
    1937–97   11
5 Retirement Hazards in the United States: a, 1960;
    b, 1970; c, 1980   45
6 Male Life and Working-Life Expectancy at Age
    Twenty, 1900–90   47
7 Female Life and Working-Life Expectancy at Age Twenty,
    1950–90   48
8 Poverty among Social Security Beneficiaries, 1999   60

Acknowledgments

This project was the brainchild of Kevin Hassett and Eric Engen, our taskmasters at the American Enterprise Institute, and we are grateful for their ideas and assistance. We are also grateful to our colleagues Julia Coronado and Thomas Glass for work on related research. Others who helped provide details on their own studies include Jeff Brown, Jeff Liebman, Alan Gustman, Karen Smith, and Thomas Steinmeier. Additional helpful comments were received from Jagadeesh Gokhale and Marvin Kosters. Finally, we want to thank Lori Stuntz and Gnomi Gouldin for help with editing the manuscript. Any remaining errors are our own.

1

Introduction

Social Security, in 1935, was intended to provide for elderly individuals without adequate sources of income. And it has a "progressive" benefit schedule that replaces a higher percentage of past earnings for those with low past earnings than for those with high past earnings. For both these reasons, the U.S. Social Security system was thought to redistribute income from rich to poor—until recently, that is. Several research teams recently developed data and models that show a more complete picture of how much the U.S. Social Security system actually redistributes income (Coronado et al. 1999, 2000, 2002; Gustman and Steinmeier 2001; Liebman 2002; Feldstein and Liebman 2002c). These papers show that Social Security is not very progressive and might even be regressive, redistributing income from poor to rich!

However, these new studies also raise many interesting questions about how to measure "progressivity," that is, the redistribution of income from rich to poor. Which data set best reflects the entire lifetime of activity necessary to capture the full effects of this life-cycle program? Is "progressivity" best measured by net dollars transferred, by net tax rates on each group, or by the internal rate of return offered by the program? What measure of "income" best reflects individuals' well-being in order to rank them from rich to poor?

Moreover, many other factors affect progressivity. First, for example, some evidence shows that the rich live longer and thus collect Social Security benefits for a longer period of time. Suppose the present value of lifetime income is used to rank everybody from rich to poor, and the present value of tax paid is subtracted from the present value of all benefits received. Then the low replacement rate of benefits given to the rich could be offset by the fact that they get those benefits for more years. That is only one example of how the system could make the rich better off at the expense of the poor.

2 INCOME REDISTRIBUTION FROM SOCIAL SECURITY

A second example relates to the treatment of the family. The Social Security system recognizes that many secondary earners remain at home raising children while providing other valuable home services such as cooking, cleaning, gardening, and home repairs. The "spousal" benefit provides some retirement income for these individuals, even though they may not pay much tax into the Social Security trust fund. In addition, Social Security's "survivor" benefit provides retirement income after the death of the primary earner. These spouses have very low measured income, yet they still receive Social Security benefits, so the system appears to redistribute toward these low-income individuals. Indeed, when studies categorize all individuals on the basis of their own earnings, Social Security looks progressive. Yet these individuals are part of a family unit, and their true well-being might better be reflected by their share of family income rather than by their own low earnings. Studies that incorporate a measure of income of this type show that some of these spousal and survivor benefits are going to rich individuals. Social Security looks less progressive and maybe even regressive.

A third example stems from another problem with measuring "income." Initial calculations were based primarily on the actual earnings of each individual (whether sharing within the family or not). As previously described, however, any individual who works at home provides valuable services that raise the level of well-being. This work does not show up as part of measured income because it is not a market transaction with dollars changing hands. However, a proper measure of well-being should not be affected by the choice of whether to work at home or for someone else. Therefore, several studies have chosen to impute some measure of "potential" earnings to each individual: what could be earned if the individual were to work full time for his whole life. The effect of this change is to move some individuals from a low actual-earnings group to a higher potential-income group, and the Social Security benefits paid to this individual are no longer going to a "poor" group but to a richer group. Once again, Social Security looks less progressive and maybe even regressive.

These studies must also choose the "discount rate" used to calculate the present value of income, payroll taxes, and Social Security benefits. Most of them initially used a low 2 percent rate of discount based on assumptions about the real no-risk rate of return. Yet, for various reasons, these assumptions may not be appropriate. In addition, the market rate of return is currently higher than 2 percent. In any case, we need to see the sensitivity of the results to the choice of discount rate. A higher rate of discount places more weight on dollars paid in taxes in the first half of life and relatively less weight on benefits received during retirement. Yet the payroll tax is slightly regressive, because it applies to income only up to a wage cap, and the Social Security benefit schedule is progressive. Thus, the higher discount rate puts more weight on the regressive part of the system and less weight on the progressive part of the system.

None of these choices is unambiguous. Nobody knows what "share" of family income to attribute to each individual within the family or what income the home worker could earn if he or she worked for someone else. The "true" discount rate remains unknown. Finally, nobody knows the best way to measure how mortality is related to income, education, or well-being. As a consequence, nobody can say with certainty whether the Social Security system is progressive or regressive.

Yet, the answer to this question is crucial for informed policymaking, especially now, as legislators ponder reforms to Social Security. Doing nothing is not an option: The Social Security Administration expects the trust fund to run out of money by 2041 (U.S. Social Security Administration 2003a). The system must be reformed somehow. Many of the current proposals would scale down traditional elements of the program, replacing part of it with individual savings accounts that pay back to each individual the returns on his own contributions. Individual accounts do not "redistribute," so this kind of reform means scaling back the parts of the program that transfer money from the rich to the poor: the progressive benefit schedule, the spousal benefits, and the survivor benefits.

For all of these reasons, it is important to know as much as possible about how the current Social Security system redistributes money in practice and to whom. We may never be able to ascertain how much Social Security really helps the poor, or indeed whether it redistributes money toward people who are already well-to-do. But our society needs to make informed choices.

Therefore, this monograph does not try to provide final answers to the questions about the actual level of redistribution within the Social Security system. Instead, we review the many factors that might affect the measure

4 INCOME REDISTRIBUTION FROM SOCIAL SECURITY

of redistribution and how recent studies have dealt with these issues. The point is not to provide a critical review of past studies or to point out any bias in their results but rather to explain how these factors affect redistribution and how the gaps in our knowledge might affect our understanding of redistribution. We also show how other considerations might affect the analysis. Along the way, we highlight what needs to be known: What kind of information might cause the system to look more progressive (or at least less regressive).

To prepare for this analysis, the next chapter reviews the essentials of the current Social Security system. It describes whom the system covers, tax rates, what income is subject to the tax, who bears the burden of the payroll tax, and how income taxes affect the Social Security system. Chapter 2 also describes the progressive benefit schedule, choices about retirement age, eligibility requirements, and spousal and survivors' benefits. Chapter 3 reviews the essentials of the studies that tried to measure the actual redistribution in the system. It discusses the different data sets employed in the literature, including both aggregate or stylized data and microdata on many individuals, as well as the different definitions or measures of *redistribution*. These variations often mean that the results are not comparable across the different studies, and we try to explain how these necessary choices might affect the analysis.

After those preliminaries, chapter 4 then lists at least seven "factors" that can affect the measure of redistribution, including (1) income-related mortality; (2) the different measures of income; (3) the coverage and rate of the Social Security payroll tax; (4) the discount rate; (5) the retirement age, including eligibility, actual trends, and relationship to socioeconomic status; (6) the choice of cohort analyzed; and (7) behavioral effects, including how Social Security rules can induce changes in the choice of how much to earn, how much to save, and when to retire.

Finally, chapter 5 concludes with a summary of our findings and a look ahead. The key findings of this monograph are research strategies needed to get a better picture of whether the Social Security system provides a significant safety net to the poor.

2

The Social Security System

Taxes

Coverage. Since the inception of Social Security in 1935, three factors have determined an individual's Social Security tax payments: (1) whether the individual is employed in a job covered by Social Security, (2) the Social Security tax rates, and (3) the maximum amount of income subject to taxation. The Social Security law of 1935 initially limited coverage to those employed in industry and commerce. In 1937 (the first year for which data are available), Social Security covered 32.9 million workers. Coverage did not change significantly until 1950, when it was expanded to include nonfarm self-employed and regularly employed farm and domestic workers. In this same year, optional coverage was extended to state and local government employees not covered by other retirement plans and nonprofit employees (U.S. Social Security Administration 2002a).

Figure 1 shows civilian workers in jobs covered by Social Security as a percentage of the civilian labor force for 1939 through 1999. Workforce coverage increased steadily from 55.1 percent in 1939 to 96 percent in 1999. Note that the largest jump occurred after the 1950 amendment. Covered earnings as a percentage of total earnings for the years 1950–99 are depicted in figure 2. Earnings coverage increased from 59.1 percent in 1950 to 86.5 percent in 1999. Today, the only significant groups of workers not covered are some government employees with separate retirement systems and those working in the underground economy (particularly domestic service workers not reporting their earnings).

Tax Rates. Table 1 presents Social Security tax rates from 1937 to present.[1] Three tax rates are shown: (1) the tax rate on employees and employers, (2)

6 INCOME REDISTRIBUTION FROM SOCIAL SECURITY

FIGURE 1
PERCENT OF LABOR FORCE COVERED BY SOCIAL SECURITY, 1939–99

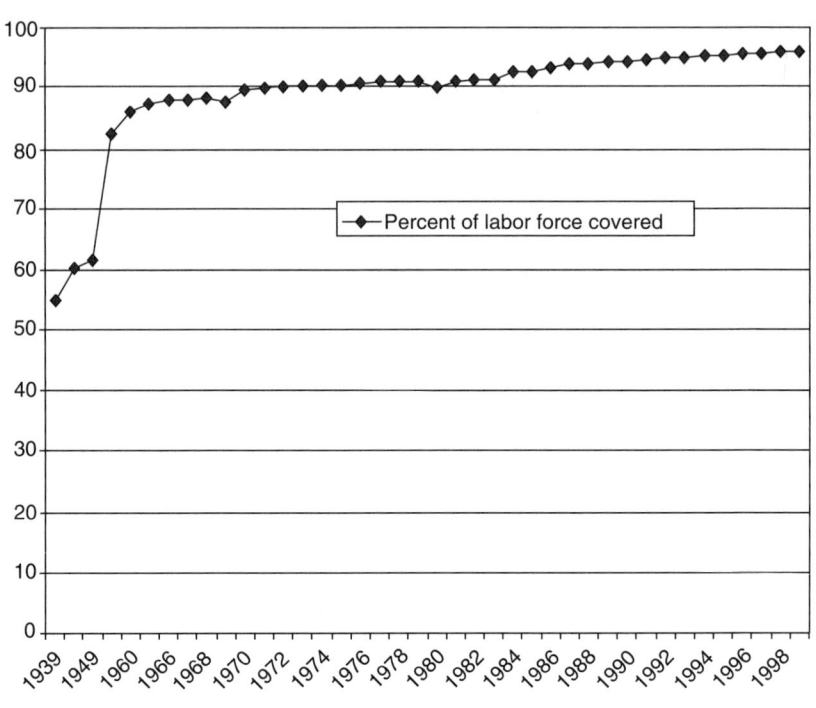

SOURCE: Committee on Ways and Means 2000, table 1-7.

the combined rate on employees and employers, and (3) the tax rate on self-employed workers. Employees and employers share Social Security payroll tax liability. Currently, both employees and employers pay the tax at a rate of 6.2 percent, so the total tax rate on this type of employment equals 12.4 percent. Social Security taxes on nonfarm self-employed workers were not instituted until 1951, when these workers first become covered. Between 1951 and 1983, tax rates on self-employment were consistently less than the combined tax rate on employees and employers. In 1978, for instance, the combined rate on employees and employers was 10.1 percent, compared to 7.1 percent on self-employment. Since 1984, however, the two types of employment have had the same total tax rates.

THE SOCIAL SECURITY SYSTEM 7

FIGURE 2
PERCENT OF EARNINGS COVERED BY SOCIAL SECURITY, 1950–99

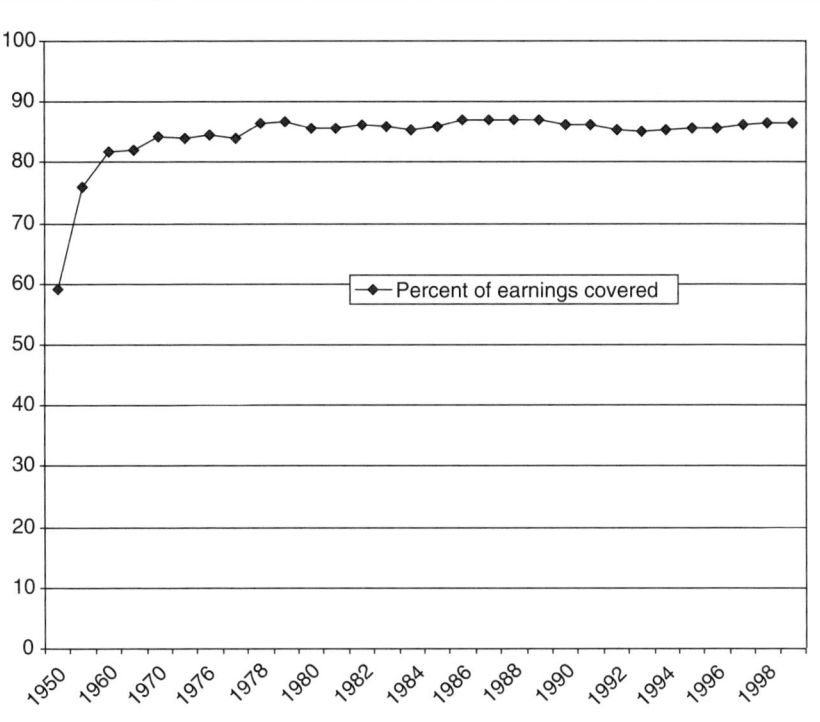

SOURCE: Committee on Ways and Means 2000, table 1-3.

Income Subject to Taxation. Table 2 displays, in nominal terms, the maximum amount of income subject to Social Security taxes from 1937 to 2002. From 1937 to 1974 and from 1979 to 1981, a statute set the maximum amount of income subject to Social Security taxes. Since 1974, an automatic adjustment determines the taxable maximum (except for 1979 to 1981). The current formula links the cap to economy-wide average wages lagged two years.[2] Figure 3 plots the maximum amount of income subject to Social Security taxes relative to average wages for the years 1951–2000. In 1951, the taxable maximum was 129 percent of average wages in the economy. The ratio decreased somewhat between 1951 and 1965, when it reached its lowest level, 103 percent. Since 1965, however, the taxable maximum has increased dramatically relative to economywide average wages. The cap

8 INCOME REDISTRIBUTION FROM SOCIAL SECURITY

TABLE 1
SOCIAL SECURITY TAX RATES AS A PERCENT OF TAXABLE EARNINGS

Calendar Year	(1) Rate for Employees and Employers	(2) Combined Tax Rate on Employees and Employers	(3) Rate for Self-Employed Persons	(4) Difference (2)–(3)
1937–49	1	2	—	—
1950	1.5	3	—	—
1951–53	1.5	3	2.25	0.75
1954–56	2	4	3	1
1957–58	2.25	4.5	3.375	1.125
1959	2.5	5	3.75	1.25
1960–61	3	6	4.5	1.5
1962	3.125	6.25	4.7	1.55
1963–65	3.625	7.25	5.4	1.85
1966	3.85	7.7	5.8	1.9
1967	3.9	7.8	5.9	1.9
1968	3.8	7.6	5.8	1.8
1969–70	4.2	8.4	6.3	2.1
1971–72	4.6	9.2	6.9	2.3
1973	4.85	9.7	7	2.7
1974–77	4.95	9.9	7	2.9
1978	5.05	10.1	7.1	3
1979–80	5.08	10.16	7.05	3.11
1981	5.35	10.7	8	2.7
1982–83	5.4	10.8	8.05	2.75
1984*	5.7	11.4	11.4	0
1985*	5.7	11.4	11.4	0
1986–87*	5.7	11.4	11.4	0
1988–89*	6.06	12.12	12.12	0
1990 and later	6.2	12.4	12.4	0

SOURCE: U.S. Social Security Administration 2002e, table 2.A3.

*In 1984 only, an immediate credit of 0.3 percent of taxable wages was allowed against the Old Age, Survivors, and Disability Insurance (OASDI) taxes paid by employees, resulting in an effective employee tax rate of 5.4 percent. The OASDI trust funds, however, received general revenue equivalent to 0.3 percent of taxable wages for 1984. Similar credits of 2.7 percent, 2.3 percent, and 2 percent were allowed against the combined OASDI and Medicare Hospital Insurance (HI) taxes on net earnings from self-employment in 1984, 1985, and 1986–89, respectively.

relative to average wages reached a peak of 255 percent in 1994. In 2000, the earnings cap was 237 percent of average wages.

The percent of covered workers with annual earnings below the taxable maximum from 1937 to 1997 is depicted in figure 4. Percentages are shown separately for men, women, and all workers. In 1937, 96.9 percent of all workers, 95.8 percent of male workers, and 99.7 percent of female

TABLE 2
MAXIMUM INCOME SUBJECT TO SOCIAL SECURITY TAXES, 1937–2002

Year(s)	Taxable Maximum	Year(s)	Taxable Maximum	Year(s)	Taxable Maximum
1937–50	3,600	1979	22,900	1992	55,500
1951–54	3,600	1980	25,900	1993	57,600
1955–58	4,200	1981	29,700	1994	60,600
1959–65	4,800	1982	32,400	1995	61,200
1966–67	6,600	1983	35,700	1996	62,700
1968–71	7,800	1984	37,800	1997	65,400
1972	9,000	1985	39,600	1998	68,400
1973	10,800	1986	42,000	1999	72,600
1974	13,200	1987	43,800	2000	76,200
1975	14,100	1988	45,000	2001	80,400
1976	15,300	1989	48,000	2002	84,900
1977	16,500	1990	51,300		
1978	17,700	1991	53,400		

SOURCE: U.S. Social Security Administration 2002e, table 2.A3.

workers had taxable earnings below the $3,000 cap. By 1965, these percentages had decreased to 63.9 percent for all workers, 51 percent of male workers, and 87.3 percent for female workers. Since 1965, however, the percentage of workers with earnings below the cap has increased along with the ratio of the taxable maximum to average wages. By 1997, 93.7 percent of all workers, 90.3 percent of male workers, and 97.6 percent of female workers had taxable earnings below the cap of $65,400.

Many consider the Social Security payroll tax to be regressive because, as income rises above the cap, the average tax rate declines. Consider two workers, earning $50,000 and $100,000 in 2002. The $50,000 earner is subject to a 12.4 percent Social Security payroll tax on his or her entire earnings. Meanwhile, the $100,000 earner pays a 12.4 percent tax rate on the first $84,900 but owes no tax on the remaining $15,100. Therefore the $100,000 earner pays an average tax rate of 10.5 percent [(0.124 × $84,900)/$100,000]. Thus, the worker with less income faces a higher average tax than the worker with more income, and Social Security payments appear to be regressive. In isolation, increases in the taxable maximum relative to average earnings are expected to make Social Security more progressive (by making the tax less regressive).

10 INCOME REDISTRIBUTION FROM SOCIAL SECURITY

FIGURE 3
TAXABLE MAXIMUM WAGES RELATIVE TO AVERAGE WAGES, 1951–2000

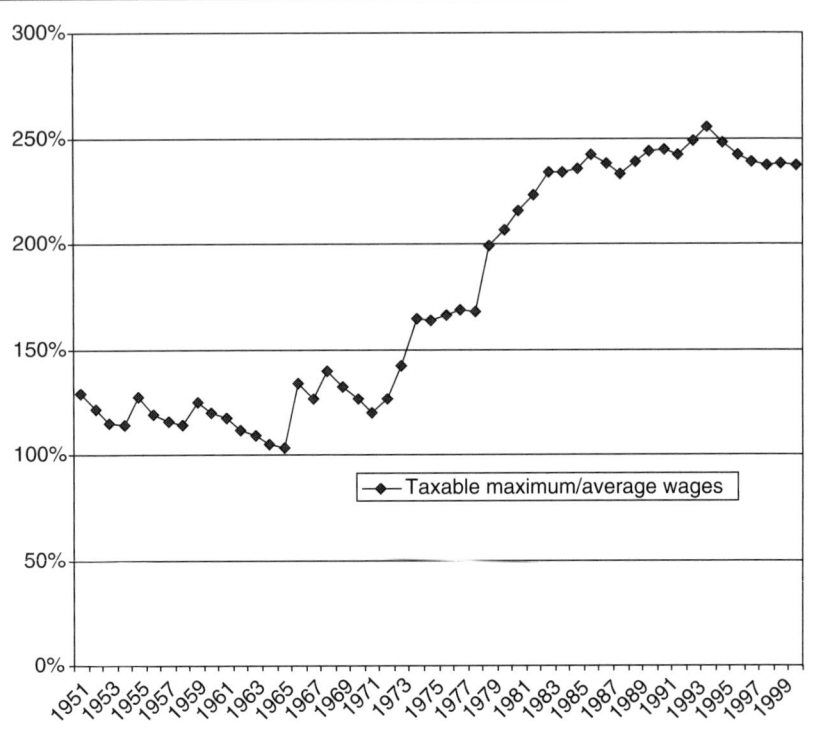

SOURCE: U.S. Social Security Administration 2002e, table 4.B1.

Tax Incidence. Tax incidence indicates how the economic burden of a tax is distributed. A fundamental principle of public finance is that this burden (economic incidence) is not determined by the party responsible for payment (statutory incidence). Instead, economic incidence is a function of the relative price responsiveness of the parties affected by the tax. In general, the parties least sensitive to price changes tend to bear a relatively large share of tax costs. Progressivity studies of Social Security (Coronado et al. 2000; Gustman and Steinmeier 2001; Liebman 2002) usually assume wage and salary workers incur the full cost of both portions of Social Security payroll taxes on employees and employers, even though the legal obligation is equally divided between workers and employers. This assumption is based on empirical evidence indicating

THE SOCIAL SECURITY SYSTEM 11

FIGURE 4
PERCENT OF WORKERS WITH EARNINGS BELOW
TAXABLE MAXIMUM, 1937–97

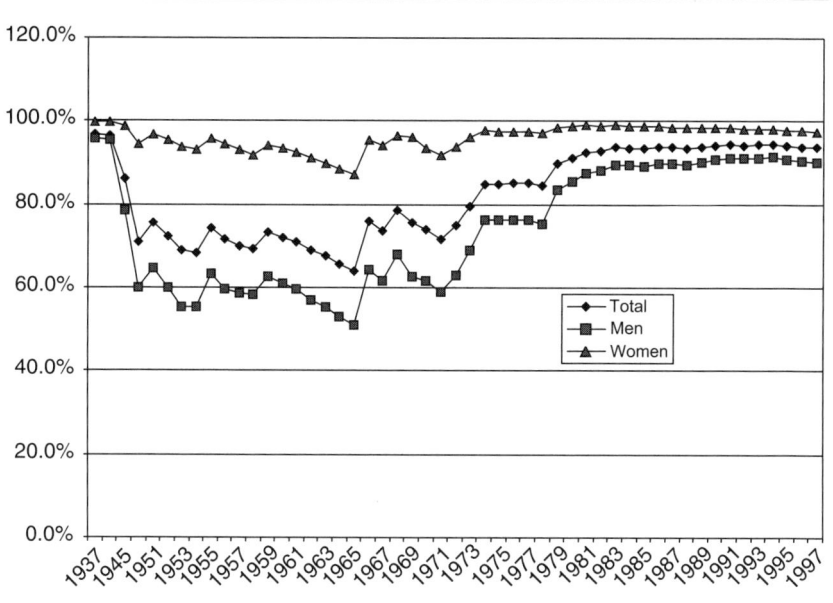

SOURCE: U.S. Social Security Administration 2002e, table 4.B4.

U.S. workers incur most of the burden of payroll taxes (see Hamermesh and Rees 1993 for a review).

Income Taxes. Panis and Lillard (1996) note that, because employer tax payments are not subject to income taxes, the net cost of the Social Security tax is less than the full Social Security payroll tax. Note that payroll taxes for self-employed workers also receive favorable income tax treatment. In addition, Social Security benefits for some beneficiaries have been subject to income taxation.

Progressivity studies of Social Security generally ignore both the income-tax deductibility of Social Security payroll taxes and income taxes on Social Security benefits. While Diamond and Gruber (1999) make calculations based on whether Social Security benefits are subject to taxation, they estimate the impact of Social Security on retirement ages, not on income

12 INCOME REDISTRIBUTION FROM SOCIAL SECURITY

TABLE 3
FULL RETIREMENT AGE AND EARLY RETIREMENT REDUCTIONS

Birth Year	Full Retirement Age	Age 62 Reduction Months	Monthly % Reductions	Total Reduction
1937	65	36	0.555	20
1938	65 and 2 months	38	0.548	20.83
1939	65 and 4 months	40	0.541	21.67
1940	65 and 6 months	42	0.535	22.5
1941	65 and 8 months	44	0.53	23.33
1942	65 and 10 months	46	0.525	24.17
1943–54	66	48	0.52	25
1955	66 and 2 months	50	0.516	25.84
1956	66 and 4 months	52	0.512	26.66
1957	66 and 6 months	54	0.509	27.5
1958	66 and 8 months	56	0.505	28.33
1959	66 and 10 months	58	0.502	29.17
1960 or later	67	60	0.5	30

SOURCE: U.S. Social Security Administration 2004, table V.C3.

inequality. Ignoring taxes other than the Social Security payroll tax may seem reasonable if the objective is to estimate redistribution from Social Security, but not other government programs such as the income tax. Yet, as discussed in chapter 4, ignoring taxes and transfers other than Social Security can lead to a distorted view of the socioeconomic status of Social Security beneficiaries. From a policy perspective, we should be interested in the impact of Social Security on economic well-being (not gross income).

Benefits

Retirement Age. Table 3 shows the full retirement age (FRA) at which full Social Security benefits can be received and reductions in benefits for early retirement by birth year. Until 2000, the FRA for Social Security was sixty-five for all birth cohorts. The 1983 Social Security amendments gradually increased the FRA in two-month increments from sixty-five for those born before 1938, to sixty-seven for those born after 1959. In 1956, early retirement benefits were introduced for women; early retirement benefits for men were enacted in 1961. While the FRA increased from sixty-five to sixty-seven, the early retirement age of sixty-two has not changed. Early retirement benefits are available at age sixty-two with a reduction in benefits for each month prior to FRA.[3] For instance, for a person born in 1950, the FRA is sixty-six and benefits are reduced for early retirement by 520 percent for each month prior to age sixty-six. For those born in 1950 and retiring at age sixty-two, benefits would be reduced by a total of 25 percent (0.520 percent per month × 48 months). In addition to reductions for early retirement, Social Security recipients also receive credits for delayed retirement. The credit is currently being increased incrementally until 2009, when it will reach a maximum of 8 percent per year.

Eligibility. In addition to changes in retirement ages, other changes in Social Security benefit eligibility have occurred since the program's inception in 1935.[4] In 1937, dependent and survivor benefits were enacted for women and children. Similar benefits for husbands and widowers were introduced in 1950. Divorced wives from marriages lasting at least ten years became eligible for benefits in 1965, while Social Security benefits for divorced husbands became available in 1983. Disabled workers over age fifty became eligible in 1956, and the age restriction on disabled workers was removed in 1960.

Benefit Formula. For the first few years of the program, recipients received lump-sum Social Security payments on retirement. Monthly benefits were first introduced in 1940. Cost-of-living adjustments (COLAs) were not introduced until 1950, when benefits were increased 77 percent. Automatic COLAs first took effect in 1975, based on changes in consumer prices. Social Security benefits can also be subject to an "earnings test." Before 2000, benefits were reduced for those with other income, but the earnings test for recipients ages sixty-five and older was eliminated in 2000. For Social Security recipients ages sixty-two to sixty-four, one dollar is still withheld for every two dollars above a threshold amount ($10,800 in 2000). Recipients subject to earnings test reductions receive delayed credits.

Currently, Social Security "benefits are calculated by indexing earnings to average wage growth (through the year the worker turns 60),

14 INCOME REDISTRIBUTION FROM SOCIAL SECURITY

summing the highest 35 years, and then dividing by 420 (35 × 12) to produce a worker's Average Indexed Monthly Earnings (AIME)" (Liebman 2002, 16).

The Social Security monthly benefit is called a *primary insurance amount* (PIA). If the individual retires at FRA, the PIA is calculated as 90 percent of AIME up to the first "bend point" ($606/month in 2003), plus 32 percent of AIME above the first bend point and up to the second bend point ($3,653/month in 2002), plus 15 percent of AIME beyond the second bend point.[5] The bend points are indexed to increase each year with average wages lagged two years.

Social Security benefits are also subject to ceilings. As of 2003, the maximum family benefit equals "150 percent of the first $774 of PIA, plus 272 percent of PIA over $774 through $1,118, plus 134 percent of PIA over $1,118 through $1,458, plus 175 percent of PIA over $1,458" (U.S. Social Security Administration 2003b, 2). The maximum monthly benefit for an individual retiring at age sixty-five in 2003 was $1,741.

Distribution of Benefits. Benefits vary widely across age and income categories. For those under age eighteen, for example, Liebman (2002, 13) estimates that benefits are twice their tax payments, "because few children have labor income, whereas some receive benefits if their parents are disabled or deceased." He also reports that current benefits received by people ages thirty to forty-nine are only 8 percent of their Social Security taxes. And yet those ages sixty-five and above receive benefits thirty times greater than their Social Security tax payments, according to Liebman (2002).

For those at retirement age, benefits also vary widely with income due to the progressive benefit schedule. The ratio of the individual's PIA to his or her AIME is called the *replacement rate*. Replacement rates at FRA are shown in table 4 for low, medium, and high earners from 1940 through 2040.[6] The progressive benefit formula means that replacement rates decrease with earnings in any year. In 1990, for instance, Social Security replaced 58.2 percent of earnings in the year prior to retirement for low earners. For medium and high earners in 1990, replacement rates were 43.2 and 24.5 percent, respectively.

Replacement rates also vary substantially across time for each earnings level. From 1940 to 1981, replacement rates increased dramatically

THE SOCIAL SECURITY SYSTEM 15

TABLE 4
SOCIAL SECURITY REPLACEMENT RATES, 1940–2040

Year	Age at Retirement	Low Earnings	Average Earnings	High Earnings
1940	65	39.4	26.2	16.5
1950	65	33.2	19.7	21.2
1960	65	49.1	33.3	29.8
1965	65	45.6	31.4	32.9
1970	65	48.5	34.3	29.2
1975	65	59.9	42.3	30.1
1976	65	60.1	43.7	32.1
1977	65	61	44.8	33.5
1978	65	63.4	46.7	34.7
1979	65	64.4	48.1	36.1
1980	65	68.1	51.1	32.5
1981	65	72.5	54.4	33.4
1982	65	65.8	48.7	28.6
1983	65	63.5	45.8	26.3
1984	65	62.6	42.8	23.7
1985	65	61.1	40.9	22.8
1986	65	60.3	41.1	23.1
1987	65	59.5	41.2	22.6
1988	65	58.4	40.9	23
1989	65	57.9	41.6	24.1
1990	65	58.2	43.2	24.5
2000	65	52.8	39.2	23.7
2010	66	56.6	42.2	27.1
2020	66 and 2 months	56.4	41.9	27.6
2030	67	56.2	41.9	27.5
2040	67	56.2	41.9	27.5

SOURCE: Committee on Ways and Means 2000, table 1-7.

for all earnings categories. For medium earners, replacement rates increased from 26.2 to 54.4 percent over this time. This trend reverses after 1981, however. By 2000, replacement rates are substantially lower than in 1981 but still higher than in 1940. For low earners, replacement rates were 52.8 percent in 2000, compared to 72.5 percent in 1981, and 39.4 percent in 1940. After 2000, replacement rates again increase slightly, but note that the FRA increases as well after 2000. For high earners, replacement rates are projected to be 27.5 percent in 2040 when retiring at age sixty-seven, compared to 23.7 percent for those retiring at age sixty-five in 2000.

16 INCOME REDISTRIBUTION FROM SOCIAL SECURITY

Because replacement rates decrease with earnings, the Social Security benefit schedule has often been characterized as redistributing income from higher-income to lower-income workers. Numerous factors other than the benefit formula affect the actual amount of redistribution in the Social Security program, however. In particular, seven key factors may influence empirical calculations of Social Security's progressivity: (1) mortality differences across workers, (2) the income measure analyzed, (3) Social Security taxes, (4) the interest rate chosen, (5) differences across workers in the retirement age, (6) the cohort analyzed, and (7) changes in behavior due to Social Security policies.

Each of these seven factors affecting progressivity estimates are considered in detail in chapter 4. Different studies controlled for these factors in varying degrees, and some factors have not been considered by any researchers to date. We review existing studies to discuss how they control for factors other than the benefit formula that affect redistribution.

3

Differences in Studies That Measure Redistribution

Data

Aggregate versus Microdata. Many past progressivity studies used aggregate or stylized data for select groups of workers with similar lifetime earnings and other characteristics.[7] Steuerle and Bakija (1994), for instance, examine cohorts of single and married workers with low, average, and high lifetime earnings reaching age sixty-five between 1940 and 2050. They assume the same stable uninterrupted earnings pattern from age twenty-one to normal retirement for each stylized earnings group. And, yet, "the fact is that essentially no Americans experience the kinds of smooth and consistent earnings trajectories assumed by Steuerle and Bakija" and others (Caldwell et al. 1999, 116). In fact, Bosworth et al. (1999, 17) estimate that "less than 14 percent of workers have the rising, humped pattern of earnings considered to be normal."

Steuerle and Bakija (1994) do not allow for changing marital status due to divorce and remarriage. By assuming workers do not divorce or remarry, this approach ignores a source of variation in Social Security that is becoming increasingly important over time with respect to redistribution (Caldwell et al. 1999; Smith et al. 2001).

As such, numerous recent articles examine Social Security's progressivity with micro simulation models accounting for heterogeneity among individuals with similar average lifetime income (Bosworth et al. 1999; Caldwell et al. 1999; Coronado et al. 1999, 2000, 2002; Brown 2002; Gustman and Steinmeier 2001; Smith et al. 2001; Liebman 2002). These recent approaches to estimating redistribution via micro simulations are the main focus of our study.

Data Sets in Micro Simulation Studies. Caldwell et al. (1999) employ the CORSIM dynamic micro simulation model of the U.S. population. This data set uses the Public-Use Microdata Sample from the 1960 Census as a beginning population. The CORSIM model "grows" this sample over time. "Specifically, it ages, marries, divorces, fertilizes, educates, employs, unemploys, re-employs, retires, and kills original sample members and their descendants over the period 1960 through 2090" (Caldwell et al. 1999, 111). Thus, the approach used by Caldwell et al. relies almost entirely on synthetic data.

Other studies using longitudinal surveys rely much less on imputations (Bosworth et al. 1999; Coronado et al. 1999, 2000; Gustman and Steinmeier 2001; Liebman 2002; Smith et al. 2001). For instance, Bosworth et al. (1999) perform micro simulations to estimate future Social Security benefits for individuals born between 1931 and 1960. Specifically, they employ the Survey of Income and Program Participation (SIPP) data for 1990–93 panels matched to Social Security Administration (SSA) earnings records for those born in 1926–65.

Liebman (2002) employs data from the 1990–91 SIPP panels, also matched to SSA earnings records. Liebman performs simulations for the 1925–29 birth cohort. Smith et al. (2001) employ the SSA's Modeling Income in the Near Term (MINT) simulation model. Just like the data used by Bosworth et al. (1999) and Liebman (2002), the MINT data are based on SIPP data matched to SSA earnings records. Smith et al. (2001) analyze MINT data for the same cohorts analyzed by Bosworth et al. (1999). One major difference between the data analyzed by Bosworth et al. (1999) and Smith et al. (2001) is that the latter differentiate mortality according to socioeconomic status. The importance of this distinction is discussed in chapter 4.

SSA earnings records contain data only on earnings subject to Social Security taxes. In 2002, for instance, income above $84,900 was not subject to the Social Security payroll tax. As discussed in greater detail in chapter 4, estimates of Social Security's progressivity can depend on whether one considers all earnings or only earnings subject to Social Security taxes. For example, Coronado et al. (2000) calculate that Social Security is slightly less progressive when estimates are based on total income than when based only on covered earnings.

Studies such as Bosworth et al. (1999) and Liebman (2002) that rely solely on SSA records for earnings data must either (1) base progressivity estimates solely on covered earnings or (2) impute earnings not subject to Social Security taxes. Bosworth et al. (1999, 9) estimate "expected earnings above the taxable maximum, but below a hypothetical ceiling" to reflect a consistent degree of censoring due to the taxable maximum. Liebman (2002), on the other hand, bases his progressivity estimates only on covered earnings.

Gustman and Steinmeier (2001) perform micro simulations based on Health and Retirement Study (HRS) data matched to SSA earnings records. They analyze HRS data for a cohort born from 1931 to 1941 matched to SSA records for 1951 to 1991. They estimate redistribution initially based on total earnings. Although Gustman and Steinmeier use SSA earnings records, they also employ HRS earnings records with data above the taxable ceiling for some workers. Unlike most micro simulation studies, Coronado et al. (2000) do not employ SSA earnings data. Instead, they estimate progressivity using Panel Study of Income Dynamics (PSID) data for the years 1968–89, which contain data on total earnings.

Measures of Redistribution

Income Comparisons. In general, we measure redistribution from Social Security by comparing the Social Security experiences of recipients with different incomes. A common method of making comparisons across income levels is to subdivide recipients by income quintile (Liebman 2002, Smith et al. 2001) or decile (Gustman and Steinmeier 2001). The first income quintile (decile) includes the lowest 20 (10) percent of earners when they are ranked by income, and the last income quintile (decile) includes the top 20 (10) percent of earners.

Instead of making comparisons across discrete income categories, Coronado et al. (2000) employ a Lorenz curve, which is a continuous measure of income distribution. They construct the Lorenz curve by first ranking every individual from lowest to highest income. Next, for each successive individual, they compute cumulative income and cumulative population. The Lorenz curve plots the cumulative percentage of income on the Y axis against the cumulative percentage of population on the X axis. Both the X and Y axes have bounds from 0 to 1 (or 0 percent to 100 percent), and the Lorenz curve lies in a box with area equal to 1. If all individuals had identical incomes, the Lorenz curve would be the 45 degree line from the bottom left corner to the upper right corner. If not, then the Lorenz curve starts out below the 45 degree line (because the poorest person of a population size N has less than $1/N$ of total income).

Absolute Redistribution Measures. Redistribution measures are broadly defined by two categories: (1) absolute measures of redistribution and (2) relative measures of redistribution. Absolute measures indicate the total amount of benefits redistributed to a given group of beneficiaries. For example, based on 1968–90 PSID data, Panis and Lillard (1996) estimate average transfers of $50,000 from men to women, $10,000 from blacks to whites, and $30,000 from high-wage to low-wage beneficiaries (based on their definition). Gustman and Steinmeier (2001) calculate similar redistributed amounts.

Relative Redistribution Measures. More commonly reported than absolute measures, relative measures gauge redistribution in relation to another variable. For example, Smith et al. (2001), Gustman and Steinmeier (2001), and Liebman (2002) compute *net transfers* or *net redistribution* from Social Security, a concept that measures lifetime benefits minus lifetime taxes. The net transfer to a particular income group "compares actual benefits of the group to the benefits that would have been received if benefits were simply pro-rated to taxes for the entire population" (Gustman and Steinmeier 2001, 17). Therefore, these net transfers must sum to zero. A system is deemed more progressive if it has larger net transfers to low-income recipients.

Another metric of redistribution based on lifetime benefits relative to lifetime taxes is the *internal rate of return* (Bosworth et al. 1999; Gustman and Steinmeier 2001; Liebman 2002). Given the timing of taxes paid and benefits received, the internal rate of return is the rate of return that an individual (or group) receives on all his or her tax payments. Gustman and Steinmeier (2001, 17) also estimate redistribution based on *share of total benefits redistributed*, which "expresses the net redistribution to the group as a percentage of the total benefits for all individuals." Coronado et al. (1999, 2000), Smith et al. (2001), and Liebman (2002) compute *net tax rates*, which equal net transfers divided by lifetime income.

Coronado et al. (2000) compute *Gini indices* before and after redistribution. The Gini index is defined as the area between the equal income line (the 45 degree line) and the Lorenz curve, divided by the area beneath the equal income line (which is $1/2$). They use the before and after Gini indices to compute the *effective progression* measure of Musgrave and Thin (1948). This equals the ratio $(1 - \text{Gini}_{AT})/(1 - \text{Gini}_{BT})$, where Gini_{BT} and Gini_{AT} are the before-tax and after-tax Gini indices, respectively. A value greater than 1 indicates a progressive system, while a value below 1 indicates a regressive system.

4

Seven Factors That Affect Redistribution

In this chapter, we discuss seven different factors that can affect the measurement of redistribution. All the measures in the literature require calculations of Social Security taxes paid and benefits received for every individual in the sample. To compute these amounts over the course of a lifetime, we need to know several things. Specifically, the net Social Security transfer is a function of mortality, income, tax rates, the discount rate, and the age at retirement. In addition, each birth cohort experienced changes in Social Security policy at different stages of their lives. We discuss the importance of each of these factors in turn, and examine how studies have controlled for them. We conclude this chapter with discussion of some behavioral effects that could also influence the measure of redistribution.

Differences in Mortality

This section examines how differences in mortality can affect the Social Security redistribution measure. We proceed in two steps. First, we discuss how variations in socioeconomic status can affect mortality. Then, we describe how redistribution studies incorporate mortality into their estimates.

Mortality and Socioeconomic Status. In an influential early study, Kitagawa and Hauser (1973) found significant mortality differences across three measures of socioeconomic status (SES): race, education level, and income. Subsequent studies have confirmed significant relationships between life expectancy and SES (see Feinstein 1993 for a review). For instance, a recent paper by Hurd et al. (2001) documents significant relationships between mortality and income, wealth, and education.[8] Since Social Security is a defined-benefit annuity, beneficiaries with longer life expectancy tend to receive greater benefits. In general, higher-income workers receive benefits for a longer period of time than their lower-income counterparts. Therefore, differences in life expectancy across income groups tend to decrease the progressivity of Social Security.

Of course, increasing income per se may not be expected to increase life expectancy. For example, "over time, in the United States and Britain, there is no stable relationship between the growth of income and the decline of mortality rates" (Deaton 2001, 16). Deaton and Paxson (2001, abstract) find "no evidence that income has any effect on mortality in Britain." The direction of causality between income and mortality is also ambiguous. Low income might lead to poor health and reduced life expectancy. "However, it is also true that individuals in poor health may be unable to earn a high income, in which case the causality of the relationship is reversed. As a result, it is quite difficult to provide any causal interpretation to the coefficient in a simple regression of mortality rates on current income" (Brown 2002, 406).

And yet, numerous variables correlated with income may contribute to differences in mortality across income groups.[9] For instance, it is well documented that women have longer life expectancies than men. Men born in the United States in 1998 are expected to live 73.8 years, while women are expected to live 79.5 (U.S. Centers for Disease Control 2002b). It is also well documented that women, on average, earn less than their male counterparts. In 1999, median full-time male earnings were $36,476 compared to $26,324 for women (U.S. Census Bureau 2002a). Therefore, women tend to outlive men despite lower earnings.

Next, we examine several specific socioeconomic characteristics to see how they affect earnings and mortality. These factors include education, race, marital status, behavior, and health.

Life expectancy tends to increase with education (Lantz et al. 1998; Brown 2002; Deaton and Paxson 2001; Hurd et al. 2001). Earnings tend to increase with education as well. Therefore, part of the link between education and mortality might be due to earnings but not education per se. Lantz et al. (1998, 1705), for instance, "demonstrated that the mechanism by which education was related to mortality was through its association with income."

Education might also be a better measure of lifetime resources than current annual income. So, holding current income constant, a significant relationship between education and life expectancy could still exist solely due to resources. Education could also proxy for unmeasured characteristics other than resources affecting mortality. "In particular, people who are more patient, more forward looking, and have more ability to delay gratification, are likely to be both better educated and healthier, even if the education itself plays no direct role" (Deaton 2001, 15). "On the other hand, there could be a very direct effect of education on mortality, if for example, more highly educated individuals better understand the risks of certain behaviors and avoid them as a result" (Brown 2002, 405).[10]

Mortality also differs significantly by race or ethnic group, as measured by age-adjusted death rates.[11] In 1998, these death rates per 100,000 people from heart disease in the United States were 211.8 for black non-Hispanics, compared to 145.3 for white non-Hispanics, 101.5 for Hispanics, 106 for American Indians, and 78 for Asians (Keppel et al. 2002). Black non-Hispanics also have higher rates of death from stroke, lung cancer, breast cancer, and homicide compared to other racial/ethnic groups in the United States. Blacks also tend to have higher mortality than whites, holding SES constant (Fuchs et al. 2001).[12]

Limited evidence is available on the relationship between Hispanic status and mortality.[13] Keppel et al. (2002) estimate that Hispanics have lower age-adjusted death rates than white non-Hispanics. They also report lower age-adjusted death rates from heart disease, stroke, lung cancer, breast cancer, and suicide for Hispanics relative to white non-Hispanics. However, non-Hispanic whites were estimated to have much lower rates of death from homicide than Hispanics. Brown (2002) and Sorlie et al. (1993) also find that Hispanics in the United States have higher life expectancy than white non-Hispanics, despite the lower SES of Hispanics. "However, there are several reasons to suspect that some of the observed difference is not real but, rather, due to sampling bias" (Brown 2002, 404). For instance, this might be true if less healthy Hispanics (such as migrant workers) are undersampled or if some Hispanic immigrants return to their birth country before dying (Pablos-Mendez 1994).

Of course, earnings also vary according to race and ethnicity. Blacks tend to have lower incomes than whites. In 1999, per-capita income for blacks in the United States was $14,397, compared to $24,109 for white non-Hispanics (U.S. Census Bureau 2002a). In the United States in 1999, Hispanic per-capita income in 1999 was $11,621, less than half the amount for non-Hispanic whites (U.S. Census Bureau 2002a).

Life expectancy may also vary with marital status (Lillard and Waite 1994; Hurd et al. 2001). Lillard and Waite find that the channels by which marriage affects mortality differ by gender. Much of the increase in life expectancy for married women is due to increases in income associated with marriage, according to Lillard and Waite. For men, they find that marital benefits are apparently due to "a settled life, improved perhaps by household management skills and labors of his wife, especially if she has at least a high school diploma" (Lillard and Waite 1994, 1154). They also find that when a marriage ends by divorce or death, men revert to the same mortality risk they faced before marriage. After divorce, women are estimated to return to the same mortality risk as those who never married. Widowed women, however, continue to enjoy reduced mortality risk even after their husbands die, according to Lillard and Waite. Hurd et al. (2001) estimate that mortality rates for married people are 21 percent lower than rates for similar singles. In sharp contrast to Lillard and Waite, Hurd et al. (2001, 195) report "no differential effect of marital status for men compared with women."

Both Lillard and Waite (1994) and Hurd et al. (2001) assume married and unmarried people are no different, once controlling for other variables such as income. Yet, "in fact, people who lead unsettled lives while married—drinking, smoking, staying out late—are probably precisely the people who are more likely to find themselves unmarried later. And those people whose married life offers the fewest benefits to them may be more likely to end a marriage and more likely to become widowed" (Lillard and Waite 1994, 1155).

The gap in life expectancy between those married and single may be partially due to high mortality rates for gay males. Hogg et al. (1997, 657) conclude that "life-expectancy at 20 for gay and bisexual men [in Vancouver] is 8 to 20 years less than for all men. If the same pattern of mortality were to continue, we estimate that nearly half of gay and bisexual men currently age twenty will not reach their 65th birthday. Under even the most liberal assumptions, gay and bisexual men in the urban centre are now experiencing life-expectancy similar to that experienced by all men in Canada in the year 1871."

Since the purpose of this section is to investigate the implications of differential mortality for the distributional effects of Social Security, we only note the possible implications for gay men in the United States. If their mortality rates are higher than for others, then Social Security redistributes away from gay males who work and pay taxes but do not receive their share of benefits, given their shorter lives.

Married people not only live longer but also tend to have higher earnings than singles. For example, in March 2000 in the United States, of men ages fifty to fifty-five earning at least $75,000, 90 percent were married with their spouse present (U.S. Census Bureau 2002b). Conversely, of the same cohort earning $15,000–$24,999, only 69 percent were married with their spouse present. Loh (1996) controls for factors other than marriage that affect earnings (such as education and experience) and estimates that married workers earn 14.8 percent more than unmarried workers. Similarly, Allegretto and Arthur (2001) estimate a marriage earnings premium of 14.1 percent.

The cause of the difference in earnings between married and unmarried workers remains unclear.[14] One possible explanation is that more productive workers are more able to attract spouses. Thus, compared to unmarried workers, married workers are "inherently more productive" (Allegretto and Arthur 2001, 632). The marriage earnings premium might also be due to a marital division of labor. This theory attributes the productivity of married workers to the specialization of tasks within the family. Marital status might also signal "to employers that other more important and fundamental properties are present in the employee. More specifically, economists often use marital status as a proxy for such personality traits as stability and responsibility" (Allegretto and Arthur 2001, 632).

Earning penalties for singles might also partially reflect labor market penalties for homosexuals, although gays and lesbians are often noted as having above-average incomes. For example, "Homosexual households had an average income of $55,400 compared with a national average of $36,500" (Broadus 1994; quoted in Badgett 1997, 65).

Badgett (1997, 1998, 2001) argues that such statistics result from unrepresentative samples. Analyzing data from the General Social Survey, she finds that "behaviorally [lesbian, gay, and bisexual] people who work full time earn less on average than behaviorally heterosexual people, even before adjusting for other differences. Lesbians earn an average of $15,056 per year compared with the $18,341 earned by the average heterosexual woman. Gay men earned $26,361, in contrast to the $28,312 earned on average by heterosexual men" (Badgett 1997, 69).

Homosexuals may fare even worse after adjusting for productivity differences. Reviewing twenty surveys from 1980 to 1991, Badgett et al. (1992) conclude that 16–44 percent of homosexuals reported employment discrimination. Badgett (1995) estimated that gay or bisexual men earn 11–27 percent less than similarly productive heterosexual men. She found little difference in earnings between lesbians and heterosexual women, however. Her sample from the General Social Survey included married and unmarried homosexual/bisexuals, but she did not disentangle the effect of marriage from the effect of homosexuality.

Allegretto and Arthur (2001) decompose the single-male earnings penalty into penalties for being a single heterosexual male and a gay male living with an unmarried male partner. Using data from the 1990 census, they estimate that "gay men in unmarried partnered relationships . . . are estimated to have earned 15.6 percent less than similarly qualified married heterosexual men, and 2.4 percent less than similarly qualified unmarried heterosexual men" (Allegretto and Arthur 2001, 631). Therefore, Allegretto and Arthur (2001) argue that most of the male single earnings penalty is due to marital status, not sexual orientation.

Behavioral characteristics can also affect mortality. For instance, smoking and obesity are correlated with increased mortality (Deaton and Paxson 2001, Fuchs et al. 2001). Of the U.S. population over age eighteen in 2000, 23.2 percent smoked, and 20.1 percent were obese (U.S. Centers for Disease Control 2002a). Life expectancy can be affected by factors that vary with socioeconomic status, such as smoking, obesity, and alcohol and drug consumption (Saffer and Chaloupka 1999). Most HIV infections result from risky behavior, and HIV is also more prevalent among lower SES groups. Of new HIV infections in the United States, 54 percent occur among blacks and 19 percent among Hispanics (Centers for Disease Control 2002a).

28 INCOME REDISTRIBUTION FROM SOCIAL SECURITY

Mortality may also vary with medical care. For instance, Fuchs et al. (2001) find that health care utilization is negatively related to mortality, after controlling for income and other measures of SES, and positively correlated with income in the United States (Fuchs et al. 2001). Thus, higher income groups seek more medical assistance, which causes an increase in life expectancy (decrease in mortality).

Mortality and Social Security Redistribution Studies. Those who live longer tend to belong to higher income groups, receive larger Social Security benefits, and collect those benefits for a longer period of time. Due to this relationship between life expectancy and income, estimates of Social Security benefits, and thus redistribution, depend crucially on controls for mortality variation.

Redistribution studies such as Bosworth et al. (1999) do not control for any life-expectancy differences due to resources. Bosworth et al. (1999, 25) conclude that the current "Social Security system favors those groups that would receive the least under an individual account system, specifically, low income earners, women, and one-earner couples." They assume, however, that workers of the same birth cohort and gender have the same life expectancy, regardless of income. Thus, their finding that the current system favors low-income earners is questionable.

Some studies have controlled for direct effects of resources on life expectancy. Adjusting life expectancy for differences in "annual income would imply that an individual with a steeply hump-shaped earnings profile would have a probability of dying that falls dramatically during high-annual-income years and then rises again during low-annual-income years" (Coronado et al. 2000, 9). Therefore, studies such as Coronado et al. (2000), Gustman and Steinmeier (2001), and Smith et al. (2001) adjust for mortality differences according to lifetime income (as opposed to annual income).

Coronado et al. (2000) estimate progressivity using Panel Study of Income Dynamics data for the years 1968–89. They present estimates based on standard mortality estimates (differentiated by age, race, and gender) and mortality differentiated by lifetime income. They compute income-differentiated life expectancy based on estimates by Sorlie et al. (1992). Coronado et al. (2000, 24) find that, after accounting for mortality differences due to lifetime income, "much of the remaining progressivity of the system appears to come in the form of spousal and survivor's benefits, while the structure in place for primary earners seems to be almost regressive. The treatment of secondary earners balances that of primary earners, and the overall system appears to be basically neutral with respect to lifetime resources."

Gustman and Steinmeier (2001) examine redistribution from Social Security using Health and Retirement Survey data matched to SSA records for those born from 1931 to 1941. They use age- and gender-specific mortality tables from the SSA adjusted for household lifetime earnings as in Duleep (1989). They estimate that redistribution decreases substantially when mortality is differentiated according to lifetime income. For instance, Gustman and Steinmeier (2001) estimate that 4.6 percent of Social Security benefits are redistributed across families with different potential earnings when mortality is not adjusted for income, while only an estimated 2.5 percent of benefits are redistributed when mortality is differentiated by income.

Perhaps the most complete mortality adjustments by researchers estimating Social Security's progressivity are by Smith et al. (2001). As in Bosworth et al. (1999), the cohorts analyzed are those born from 1931–35 through 1956–60. Unlike Bosworth et al., Smith et al. (2001, 7) differentiate mortality by "race, education, marital status, permanent income, calendar time, and age group."[15] They adopt mortality estimates from Panis and Lillard (1999).

Smith et al. (2001) find that mortality adjustments sharply reduce the progressivity of Social Security when income is measured by permanent income at age sixty-two. For example, for the 1931–35 birth cohorts, "net benefits from OASI [Old Age and Survivors Insurance] decline from 19 percent of income to just over 3 percent of income as income rises between the second quintile and the top quintile. But net benefits from OASI are negative in the bottom [quintile] and large, amounting to negative 18 percent of income" (Smith et al. 2001, 14). This is primarily due to shorter life expectancy for low earners. Results are similar for the 1956–60 birth cohort, except that net benefits also turn negative for the top two quintiles.

Due to the endogeneity of income, however, many researchers do not want to use income directly as a determinant of mortality. Income typically falls before death. Therefore, some choose to have mortality depend on

30 INCOME REDISTRIBUTION FROM SOCIAL SECURITY

something that does not change close to death but is correlated with income, like education. Liebman (2002), for example, adjusts mortality for differences according to sex, race, and education, although he does not adjust mortality for direct income effects. He employs mortality estimates developed by Brown et al. (2002).[16] To reflect conditions in 2075, life expectancies are scaled to be consistent with those born in 1990. He estimates that when mortality varies according to race and education, lifetime benefits in the lowest AIME quintile fall by about 2 percent, while lifetime benefits in the highest AIME quintile increase by approximately 1 percent. Liebman (2002, 34) notes that accounting for independent effects of income on life expectancy "would increase the effect of differential mortality on the benefit levels of the different income quintiles."

Brown (2002) examines redistribution via Social Security individual account annuities controlling for variation in life expectancy. Since the value of annuities increases with life expectancy, "annuities which ignore individual or group characteristics will result in expected transfers away from high-mortality risk groups to low-mortality risk groups" (Brown 2002, 402). Brown generates new estimates of mortality using data from the National Longitudinal Mortality Study (NLMS), building on work by Brown et al. (2002).[17] He constructs age-specific mortality rates by gender, race, ethnicity, and level of education. He finds that "mortality rates differ substantially across these groups, leading to very different valuations of annuities" (Brown 2002, 402). Note that Brown (2002) does not differentiate mortality by income, however. Instead, education is the only measure of resources used to differentiate mortality. While the NLMS data include a measure of income, Brown does not use this information. "This choice is driven in part by a belief that education is a better proxy for lifetime resources than other measures, and in part by necessity—the NLMS income data are of questionable value" (Brown 2002, 405).

All the studies mentioned in this section find that incorporating mortality estimates changes the measure of redistribution. Some differentiate mortality by income and others by education (which is positively correlated with income). Still, they all find that Social Security becomes more regressive (less progressive) when allowing mortality to vary by SES.

Income Measures

In this section we discuss how various issues that relate to income measurement can affect Social Security distribution estimates. Specifically, we consider eight issues: (1) aggregate versus individual income, (2) annual versus lifetime income, (3) covered versus total earnings, (4) own benefits versus spouse and survivor's benefits, (5) individual versus family income, (6) potential versus actual income, (7) gross versus net income, and (8) variations in cost of living. Each of these eight decisions made by the researcher can affect the resulting measurement of progressivity via the estimates of Social Security taxes paid, benefits received, and mortality.

Aggregate versus Individual Income. Estimates of the progressivity of Social Security depend crucially on the measure of income analyzed. Many past progressivity studies (Hurd and Shoven 1985; Boskin et al. 1987; Steuerle and Bakija 1994; Diamond and Gruber 1999) used aggregate or stylized income measures for select groups of workers with similar lifetime earnings and other characteristics.[18]

Steuerle and Bakija (1994), for instance, examine stylized cohorts of single and married workers reaching age sixty-five between 1940 and 2050. They further divide the cohorts into three categories of lifetime earnings: low, average, and high. Low earners are defined as having 45 percent of mean covered earnings, average earners are defined as having average covered earnings, and high earners are defined as having maximum taxable earnings. They assume uninterrupted earnings from age twenty-one until normal retirement age for each stylized earnings pattern. And yet,

> the fact is that essentially no Americans experience the kinds of smooth and consistent earnings trajectories assumed by Steuerle and Bakija [and others]. To begin, there is considerable variation across and within cohort members in work experience. At the macro level we see periodic recessions, changes over time in the normal rate . . . of unemployment, changes in the duration of unemployment, changes in labor force participation, a strong and ongoing trend toward early

retirement, significant changes over time in fertility rates, and, particularly among the upper income classes, a rise in the average age of first birth. Each of these macro phenomena can materially alter the amount of time members of a particular cohort spend working over the course of their lifetimes. We also know that particular members of each cohort are differentially affected by these phenomena. (Caldwell et al. 1999, 116–17)

As such, the more recent studies that examine Social Security's progressivity account for heterogeneity among individuals with similar average lifetime income (Bosworth et al. 1999; Caldwell et al. 1999; Coronado et al. 1999, 2000; Gustman and Steinmeier 2001; Brown 2002; Liebman 2002).

Annual versus Lifetime Income. McGarry (2002) and Johnson (1999) each examine the impact of Social Security redistribution on poverty among older Americans. They base their estimates solely on annual income, which may be appropriate if one is concerned primarily with the effect of the program on poverty among the elderly. Indeed, "The Committee on Economic Security of 1935 made clear these needs based progressivity goals by stressing that poverty among the elderly was the primary problem to be addressed" (Steuerle and Bakija 1994, 14). However, it is not necessary to redistribute income from wealthy retirees to keep lower-income retirees out of poverty. Participants pay taxes while working and are promised benefits upon retirement, regardless of economic circumstances. Therefore "many think of Social Security in the context of a life-cycle model" (Coronado et al. 2000, 19).

Accordingly, many recent studies that estimate redistribution from Social Security measure income on a lifetime basis. For instance, Coronado et al. (2000) estimate that Social Security is much less progressive when individuals are arrayed by lifetime earnings, as compared to estimates based on annual earnings. "The reason is that beneficiaries are not as poor as they looked using annual income. With this lifetime concept, the effect of Social Security is still progressive, but much less so" (Coronado et al. 2000, 19).

Covered Earnings versus Total Earnings. For 2002, income above $84,900 is not subject to the Social Security payroll tax. Estimates of Social Security's progressivity depend on whether one considers all earnings or only covered earnings subject to Social Security taxes. Liebman (2002), for instance, estimates redistribution from Social Security based only on earnings subject to Social Security payroll taxes. Gustman and Steinmeier (2001), on the other hand, base their progressivity estimates on total earnings. In contrast, Coronado et al. (2000) generate estimates based on both covered earnings and total earnings for comparison.

As Bosworth et al. (1999) note, censoring of earnings would be of little concern for comparisons across time if the ceiling remained fairly constant relative to average earnings. However, the ratio of the maximum amount of income subject to Social Security taxes to average earnings has fluctuated over time, as depicted for 1951–2000 in figure 3. In 1951, the taxable maximum was 129 percent of economywide average wages. The ratio decreased somewhat between 1951 and 1965, when the ratio reached a minimum of 103 percent. Yet, between 1965 and the early 1980s, the cap increased dramatically relative to average wages. In 2000, the cap was 237 percent of average wages. As such, earnings measures based only on covered earnings upwardly bias wage growth, at least for high earners (Bosworth et al. 1999). To reflect a consistent degree of censoring, they estimate "expected earnings above the taxable maximum, but below a hypothetical ceiling" (Bosworth et al. 1999, 9).

Suppose the ceiling was constant relative to average earnings. This would still affect overall progressivity, because low-income earners have a greater percentage of income subject to Social Security taxes than high-income earners. Bosworth et al. (1999), for example, estimate that less than 1 percent of women in their sample earned wages above the taxable wage ceiling. Among men at least twenty-two years old, however, they estimate that 23 percent had earnings above the tax ceiling at least once between 1984 and 1993.

In addition, workers with the same amount of lifetime income can have different amounts of income subject to Social Security taxation depending on when or where the income is earned. Gustman and Steinmeier (2000), for instance, find large differences in tax rates between natives and immigrants with similar lifetime incomes.

34 INCOME REDISTRIBUTION FROM SOCIAL SECURITY

How progressivity estimates are affected by exclusion or inclusion of income not subject to Social Security taxes depends on how progressivity is measured. For measures based on the absolute amount of redistribution, the choice of whether to include or exclude noncovered earnings matters only to the extent that it moves a person from one income category to another.

If the measure of progressivity is based on Social Security tax rates, then the inclusion of noncovered earnings could have a significant effect on results. The Social Security payroll tax is regressive by this measure, because as income rises above the cap, the average tax rate declines. Therefore, for tax-rate-based measures, estimates tend to show less progressivity when total earnings are considered compared to calculations based only on covered earnings. Coronado et al. (2000) estimate progressivity based both on lifetime earnings subject to Social Security taxes and on full lifetime income. Using a progressivity measure based on tax rates, Coronado et al. (2000) determine that Social Security is slightly less progressive when calculations are based on total income than when based on covered earnings.

Own Benefits versus Spouse and Survivor Benefits. Progressivity estimates also vary depending on the treatment of spouse or survivor benefits. The "spousal benefit" is half the worker's benefit, if that is higher than the spouse's own PIA. The survivor's benefit, however, is always the same as that of the deceased worker. Divorced individuals are eligible for ancillary benefits provided the marriage lasted at least ten years. An individual first receives benefits based on his own eligibility. Additional payments are made if the spouse or survivor benefits exceed an individual's own benefits. Therefore, a married or widowed worker receives no net Social Security benefit from paying Social Security taxes until the benefit from his own contributions exceeds the spousal or survivor's benefit.

A married woman receives no net increase in her Social Security benefit from working until the benefit from her own earnings exceeds her spousal or survivor's benefit. For a husband with a given income, a wife not in the labor force receives more net gains from Social Security than a working wife earning substantially less than her husband. Therefore, one could argue that married women who never enter the labor force with high-earning husbands receive the greatest net benefit from Social Security.

Liebman (2002) notes, however, that when considering the effect of spouse and survivor benefits, one needs to consider a specific alternative use for these revenues. He argues that if the alternative use is a *proportional* benefit increase (or proportional payroll tax decrease), spouse and survivor benefits would not affect redistribution much. If the alternative use is to increase benefits (or decrease payroll taxes) by a constant dollar *amount* for all recipients, "then spouse and survivor benefits cause substantial redistribution toward high income households" (Liebman 2002, 34). Measuring redistribution based on the fraction of total benefits redistributed, Gustman and Steinmeier (2001) estimate that transfers to lower AIME groups are reduced by approximately a third after accounting for spouse and survivor benefits.

Individual versus Family Income. Consideration of spouse and survivor benefits suggests that it may be more appropriate to measure redistribution based on family income rather than individual income (Gustman and Steinmeier 2001). Social Security seems very progressive when making comparisons across individuals. Indeed, the spousal benefit may go to a spouse that has very low earnings of his or her own. Yet, much of this redistribution occurs within families, primarily from married men to their wives, for three reasons: (1) lower earnings for women than men, (2) spousal and survivor benefits, and (3) greater life expectancy for women than men. From a policy perspective, poverty concerns are not relevant for a low-wage earner within a high-income family (Coronado et al. 2000). Therefore many studies have estimated progressivity using household resources as opposed to individual resources.

Gustman and Steinmeier (2001) find that total redistribution is slightly lower when family AIME replaces individual AIME. They estimate that transfers away from upper-income families decrease by about one-fourth, and that transfers to the third through fifth income deciles shrink by approximately two-thirds. For the very lowest income group, however, Gustman and Steinmeier (2001) find that redistribution increases by over 25 percent.

Potential versus Actual Income. Differences in lifetime earnings are due in part to individual preferences between work for pay and other activities.

Many individuals with low lifetime earnings have significant years when they did not work for pay but could have done so. Gustman and Steinmeier (2001, 22) estimate that "many of the individuals in the lowest AIME groups are women who are married to men with substantial earnings power and who have chosen to not work during substantial parts of their lives." One can argue that, when measuring redistribution, one should not include transfers between individuals with the same potential earned income, but who make different choices regarding time spent working for pay and time spent engaging in non–labor market activities (such as building one's own house, growing one's own vegetables, or taking care of one's own family).

To account for the influence of individual labor market decisions, some studies measure progressivity using potential rather than actual income. Coronado et al. (2000) define potential yearly income as the hourly wage rate multiplied by 4,000 hours. After making this adjustment, the distribution of lifetime income is more even, and "Social Security is only slightly progressive at best" (Coronado et al. 2000, 22). Of course, time spent out of the workforce may not be entirely voluntary. To account for this possibility, they also estimate potential income valuing time out of the workforce at half the wage rate. As expected, they find Social Security is more progressive when home time is valued at half the hourly wage than when valued at the full wage.

Gustman and Steinmeier (2001, 21) measure potential income by "significant earnings," which they define as the "average amount earned in years when the individual was seriously committed to work." Such an individual has "earnings [that] amount to more than 25 percent of the average of the highest 5 years of indexed earnings" (Gustman and Steinmeier 2001, 21). On average, this measure excludes about four years of earnings and more for women compared to men. Like Coronado et al. (2000), Gustman and Steinmeier find Social Security to be less progressive when using potential rather than actual income. They find that estimating progressivity based on potential earnings has little effect on transfers to the lowest income decile, even though redistribution to the other deciles is much lower. Indeed, when estimates are based on potential family earnings, "there is so little redistribution among deciles . . . [that] most of the redistribution must be within deciles. In turn, most of the redistribution within deciles defined

SEVEN FACTORS THAT AFFECT REDISTRIBUTION 37

on the basis of potential earnings must be from families with two earners to traditional families with roughly the same combined earning power but in which only one spouse is a lifetime worker" (Gustman and Steinmeier 2001, 23).

Liebman (2002) reports progressivity estimates based on the AIME of the highest earner in the household. He argues that "because most high earners work full-time for at least thirty-five years, this measure is similar to the potential earnings measures used in the studies of Coronado et al. (2000) and Gustman and Steinmeier (2001)" (Liebman 2002, 22). Compared to estimates based on total household income, he estimates that Social Security is less progressive when it is based on the AIME of the primary earner.

Gross versus Net Income. Studies have estimated progressivity either based on Social Security benefits or, more recently, based on Social Security benefits relative to Social Security payroll tax payments. In general, these studies ignore the effect of other taxes and transfers on income distribution. For instance, Social Security benefits are subject to income taxation for some recipients, although the effect of these taxes on the progressivity of Social Security is not considered. In fact, we are not aware of any progressivity studies that estimate redistribution from Social Security while accounting for taxes other than Social Security payroll taxes or transfers other than Social Security benefits.[19]

The Census Bureau claims that taxation in the United States reduces annual income inequality (U.S. Census Bureau 2001). Since Social Security payroll taxes are regressive, other types of taxes must reduce inequality in annual income. In 2000, for instance, the progressive federal individual income tax accounted for 33.2 percent of all government revenue in the United States, and 39.5 percent of revenue excluding Social Security tax revenue (U.S. Census Bureau 2002c). Transfers other than Social Security should also reduce annual income inequality. In fact, the Census Bureau estimates that both means-tested transfers and non-means-tested transfers, including Social Security, reduce inequality in annual income (U.S. Census Bureau 2001).

Inclusion of non–Social Security taxes and benefits is complicated by a couple of factors. These transfers may affect lifetime income differently than they affect annual income. In addition, the incidence of these taxes and benefits is not necessarily all on the worker, as is assumed for Social Security.

An important question, even just for studies of the progressivity of Social Security taxes and benefits, is what measure of income to use to classify households or individuals. It can be (1) income before any other taxes and transfers, (2) income before taxes but including non–Social Security transfers, or (3) income after all taxes and transfers. The first measure classifies people by actual or potential earnings power, to see how the Social Security system modifies that measure. The second differentiates people by earnings plus transfers, while the third classifies people by a measure of well-being that remains after all government redistribution, *including* Social Security taxes and benefits. All studies reviewed here chose the first measure, although we note that this choice is not ambiguous and could affect estimates of Social Security's progressivity.

Cost of Living. Previous studies base progressivity estimates on income measures that are not adjusted for cost-of-living differences. Cost of living can vary across geographic areas and over time. Consider a worker in College Station, Texas, earning $62,820, and a worker in Boston, Massachusetts, earning $100,000 in 1999. According to ACCRA price data, both workers have the same real purchasing power.[20] In 1999, the maximum amount of income subject to Social Security taxes was $72,600, and the Social Security tax rate was 12.4 percent (6.2 percent levied on each the worker and employer). Thus, the College Station worker pays Social Security taxes equal to $7,790 (12.4 percent of $62,820), while the Boston worker pays $9,002 (12.4 percent of the first $72,600 earned).[21] The College Station worker faces a 12.4 percent tax rate, although the Boston worker pays only 9 percent. Thus, for a given amount of real purchasing power, workers in low cost-of-living areas have higher taxes relative to purchasing power. This is because the Social Security payroll tax does not adjust the taxable maximum income level for cost-of-living differences.

For beneficiaries with a given amount of real lifetime purchasing power, workers in low cost-of-living areas receive greater real benefits relative to their real income. This tends to offset the higher tax rates in low cost-of-living areas. Thus, the net effect of adjusting for cost of living within each area would depend on (1) changes in the cost of living over time and

(2) the discount rate. If the net effect of these considerations is to raise the present value of Social Security taxes more than benefits in high-cost locations and the poor tend to live in high-cost areas, then existing studies may overstate the progressivity of Social Security. Otherwise, they may underestimate progressivity.

Workers are mobile—they can move from one area to another. In general, workers paying taxes in high cost-of-living areas and retiring to low cost-of-living areas receive the best "bang for their buck" from Social Security. If people with more lifetime income are more mobile and more likely to move from high to low cost-of-living areas on retirement, then standard measures overstate the true progressivity of Social Security. Conversely, if those with low incomes tend to work in high cost-of-living areas and move to lower cost-of-living areas to retire, then past studies may have underestimated progressivity. The bias in existing estimates is hard to judge.

A common problem with cost-of-living indices, however, is that they are based on prices determined by both supply and demand. People can choose where to work as well as where to retire. Accordingly, higher prices in higher cost areas partially reflect higher demand. For example, Dumond et al. (1999) estimate that metropolitan cost-of-living indices overstate real wage differentials by 60 percent, because of differences in demand across metropolitan areas. Perhaps for this reason, cost-of-living adjustments are not used in the existing literature.

Social Security Taxes

Once we have suitable mortality estimates and a measure of income for each individual, we need to calculate net Social Security transfers. An individual's Social Security tax payments are determined by (1) whether the individual is covered by Social Security, (2) Social Security tax rates, and (3) the maximum amount of income subject to taxation. We discuss the effects of all three factors in this section.

Coverage. For a detailed portrait of persons covered by Social Security since 1935, please refer to chapter 2. Note that coverage has increased significantly since the inception of the program. Therefore, it is possible for a person to work a substantial number of years in noncovered employment, paying no Social Security taxes, and still have thirty-five or more years of covered employment.

Since Social Security benefits are calculated using only the highest thirty-five years of covered earnings, workers switching from noncovered to covered employment could have lower lifetime tax payments with little or no offsetting reduction in benefits. Therefore, beneficiaries spending less time in covered employment could receive transfers from beneficiaries spending more time in covered employment due to differences in lifetime tax rates. Accordingly, if those with low income are more likely to spend less of their life in covered employment, then existing studies that consider only covered workers may underestimate the progressivity of Social Security.

Tax Rates. For a complete history of the Social Security tax rates, refer to chapter 2. Here, we briefly recall just a few key points: Employees and employers share the statutory incidence of the tax. Currently they are each taxed at a rate of 6.2 percent, for a total of 12.4 percent. From 1950, when the nonfarm self-employed first became covered, until 1984, the tax rate on the self-employed was consistently less than the combined tax rate on employees and employers. The existing redistribution studies do not include separate tax rates for self-employed workers in their calculations. For instance, Smith et al. (2001) assume that their entire sample paid the combined tax rate, although many workers in their sample are likely self-employed. To our knowledge, no researchers have calculated redistribution between self-employed and wage and salary workers.

To put the importance of self-employment in context, in 1948, the ratio of nonfarm self-employed workers to wage and salary employees was 0.121 (U.S. Bureau of Economic Analysis 2003). By 2000, this ratio had decreased to 0.079. Of course, the prevalence of self-employment would not affect Social Security's progressivity if income distributions were the same for both types of workers. Yet, on average, self-employed income is much greater than wage and salary income. In 1948, for example, per capita nonfarm self-employment income was $4,004, compared to $2,958 for wage and salary workers (U.S. Bureau of Economic Analysis 2003). In 2000, per capita nonfarm self-employment income was $75,441, compared to $41,013 for wage and salary employees (U.S. Bureau of

Economic Analysis 2001). Therefore, it is clear that the distribution of income between these types of workers is not equal.

Self-employed workers with higher average incomes than other workers (1) did not participate in Social Security until the 1950s and (2) faced reduced tax rates from 1950 to 1984. Therefore, it seems likely that, until recently, self-employment has dampened Social Security's progressivity. Studies of past progressivity, therefore, may have neglected an important factor affecting redistribution from Social Security. Bias could result from either (1) assuming self-employed workers had no earnings prior to being covered in 1950 or (2) assuming self-employed workers paid the higher combined tax rate on employees and employers from 1950 to 1984.

Amount of Income Subject to Taxation. A tax is regressive if the average tax rate (tax payments divided by income) declines with income. Since not all earnings are subject to Social Security taxes, the Social Security payroll tax is regressive. Specifically, as income rises above the earnings cap, the average Social Security tax rate declines.

Table 2 depicts the maximum amount of income subject to Social Security taxes from 1937 to 2002. The ratio between the maximum amount of income subject to Social Security taxes and average wages for the years 1951–2000 is depicted in figure 3. This ratio decreased between 1951 and 1965, reaching a minimum of 103 percent in 1965. After 1965, the ratio increased dramatically. In 2000, the taxable maximum was 237 percent of economywide average wages. In isolation, increases in the taxable maximum relative to average earnings tend to make Social Security more progressive (by making the Social Security tax less regressive).

As noted previously, progressivity estimates vary depending on whether they are based on total earnings or earnings subject to Social Security taxes. Estimates based only on covered earnings (such as Liebman 2002) effectively assume that the Social Security tax is proportional at all income levels. For example, Coronado et al. (2000) show that Social Security is slightly less progressive when they use total income as opposed to estimates that rely on covered earnings. Thus, by ignoring the regressive nature of the Social Security tax, studies basing estimates only on covered earnings tend to overestimate redistribution (at least for relative redistribution measures; see Liebman 2002 and pages 33–34 of this chapter).

Discount Rate

The discount rate provides a means of valuing in comparable monetary units all of the Social Security taxes paid and benefits received at different times. Most people value a future payment of $100 at some amount less than $100 today. If an individual would be willing to pay $95.24 today for a payment of $100 a year from now, the implied discount rate is 5 percent. It indicates that the person requires a 5 percent return on an investment in order to forgo $95.24 in current consumption for one year.

While the Social Security tax is regressive, the benefit schedule is progressive. Therefore, the progressivity of the entire system depends on how taxes paid earlier in life are valued relative to benefits received later in life. In general, the greater the discount rate, the less progressive is the overall Social Security system. Progressivity is negatively related to the discount rate, because higher discount rates mean that the later progressive benefits are weighted less relative to the earlier regressive taxes.

Researchers disagree on the choice of appropriate discount rate for estimating overall redistribution. Steuerle and Bakija (1994) and Bosworth et al. (1999) assume a 2 percent real (inflation adjusted) discount rate.[22] Liebman's (2002) main results use a 1.29 percent real discount rate. Steuerle and Bakija (1994, 100) base their choice of discount rate on average rates of return on safe investments and argue that "Social Security is an extremely safe investment that is uniquely resistant to economic fluctuations and inflation and receives favorable tax treatment." Liebman (2002) bases his choice of discount rate on the cohort rate of return to Social Security. Thus, "an individual who receives exactly the cohort rate of return on his or her Social Security taxes will have a net transfer of zero, whereas someone with a rate of return higher than that of the cohort will receive a positive transfer, and someone with a lower rate of return will receive a negative transfer" (Liebman 2002, 20).

Caldwell et al. (1999, 118) argue that studies such as Steuerle and Bakija employing low real discount rates "bias upward their estimates of Social Security's net benefits for all contributors. But they differentially bias upward their net benefit estimate for those with longer life expectancies—in this case women." They note that the real rate of return on inflation-indexed Treasury bonds is much higher than 2 percent. For instance, the current yield on thirty-year inflation-indexed treasury bonds is 3.88 percent. Caldwell et al. also argue that safe rates of return for longer maturities could be considerably higher. While the longest maturity on inflation-indexed bonds is currently 30.5 years, workers can pay Social Security taxes for considerably longer than thirty years before retiring.

Caldwell et al. (1999) also disagree with Steuerle and Bakija's (1994) assertion that Social Security is a safe investment. They argue that Social Security is risky due to changes in demographics, real wage growth, legislation, and inflation. Moreover, Caldwell et al. note that "Social Security is not a capital asset, and the tax treatments of Social Security contributions and Social Security benefits are not relevant to deciding the rate of return at which these flows should be discounted. What is relevant is the after-tax rate of return workers could otherwise receive were they able to invest their contributions in real assets" (Caldwell et al. 1999, 118).

Accordingly, some studies employ discount rates higher than the 2 percent of Steuerle and Bakija (1994) and Bosworth et al. (1999). For example, Smith et al. (2001) choose a 2.7 percent real discount rate. In addition, numerous studies use multiple discount rates to demonstrate the sensitivity of their estimates to the choice of discount factor. For example, while Caldwell et al. (1999) assume a 5 percent discount rate for most of their estimates, they also report results for 3 and 7 percent real discount rates. And, while Liebman's (2002) main estimates discount at a 1.29 real rate, he also reports estimates for 3 and 5 percent real discount rates. Liebman (2002) finds that aggregate net benefits become negative when increasing the discount rate from 1.29 to 3 percent (and even more negative when the discount rate is raised further to 5 percent). Coronado et al. (2000) estimate redistribution at 2 and 4 percent real discount rates. Like Liebman (2002), Coronado et al. (2000) also find that very few people receive positive net transfers at a higher discount rate. In addition, they calculate that Social Security is regressive when discounting at a 4 percent real rate.

For most of their estimates, Gustman and Steinmeier (2001) use actual observed interest rates to date and intermediate projections of the SSA. To test their interest rate assumption, they also employ "the social security low cost assumptions about the interest rate, which leads to a long-run [nominal] interest rate of 6.5 percent rather than 6.3 percent. This leads

44 INCOME REDISTRIBUTION FROM SOCIAL SECURITY

to a substantial reduction in the present value of benefits, . . . but redistribution patterns which are relatively unchanged" (Gustman and Steinmeier 2001, 25). Note, however, that Gustman and Steinmeier (2001) base their sensitivity analysis on a much smaller difference in interest rates (0.2 percent) compared to other studies, such as Coronado et al. (2000) and Liebman (2002). In any case, they each find that higher discount rates cause Social Security to look more regressive.

Retirement Age

Age of Eligibility. Table 3 shows the full retirement age at which full Social Security benefits can be received, according to birth year and the accompanying reductions in benefits for early retirement.[23] Monthly benefit reductions are intended to make lifetime benefits approximately equal for both early retirement and normal retirement. Of course, this would only be true for individuals with average life expectancies. In general, people with lower than average life expectancies receive a better deal from early retirement than from normal retirement, while the opposite is true for people with above-average life expectancies. In addition to the benefit reductions for early retirement, recipients can also receive credits for delayed retirement. However, these benefits are less than actuarially fair on average.

Retirement Trends. Our figure 5 originally appeared as figure 12 of Gruber and Wise (1999), which shows retirement hazard rates in 1960, 1970, and 1980. The retirement hazard rate indicates the percent of workers of a given age who retire at that age. First consider 1960, when Social Security benefits were not available for men until age sixty-five. Rates of departure from the labor force are low until age sixty-five. At this point the hazard spikes dramatically, indicating that age sixty-five was by far the most frequent retirement age in 1960. Early retirement benefits at age sixty-two first became available in 1961. By 1970, the retirement hazard at age sixty-two was much greater than it was in 1960, although sixty-five was still the most frequent retirement age. Finally, by 1980, age sixty-two was the most frequent age of retirement.

SEVEN FACTORS THAT AFFECT REDISTRIBUTION 45

FIGURE 5
RETIREMENT HAZARDS IN THE UNITED STATES: A, 1960; B, 1970; C, 1980

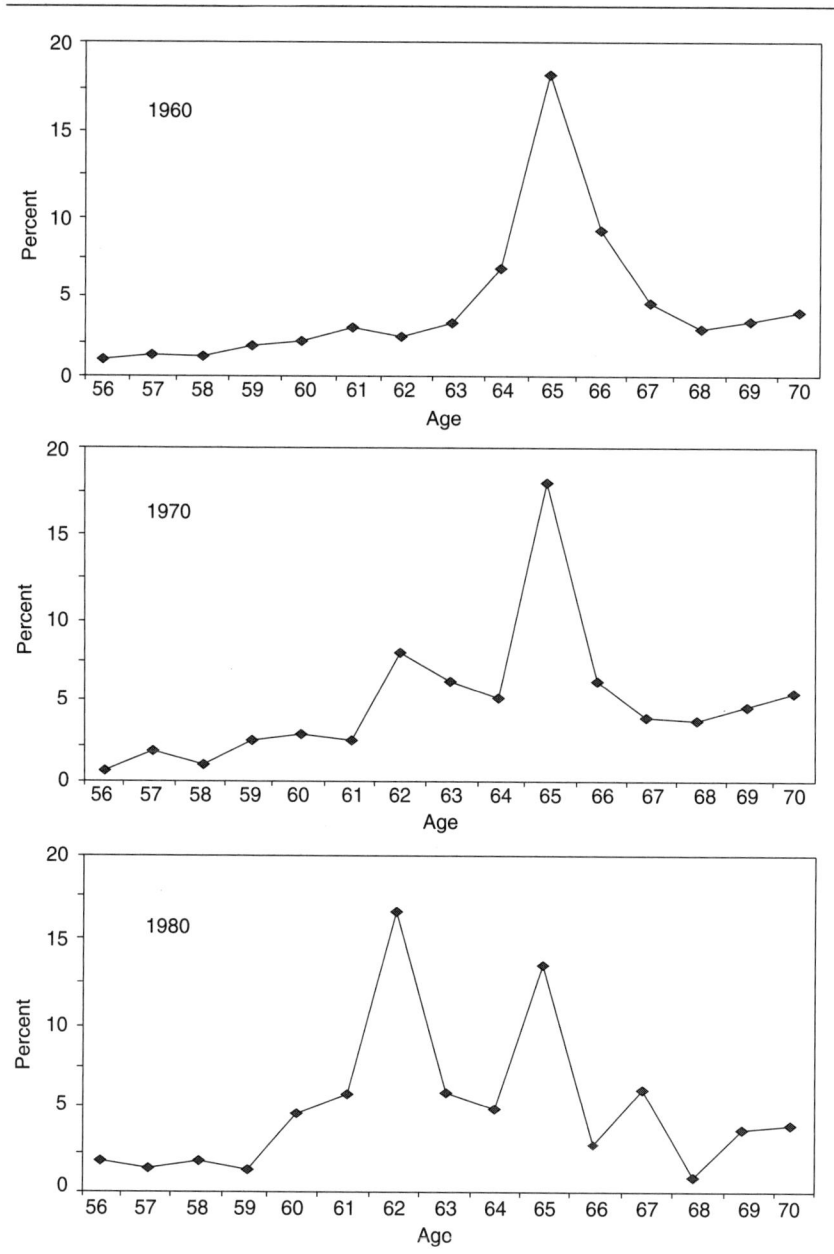

SOURCE: Gruber and Wise 1999, 17, using data from Burtless and Moffitt 1984.

46 INCOME REDISTRIBUTION FROM SOCIAL SECURITY

TABLE 5
AVERAGE RETIREMENT AGE AND EXPECTED RETIREMENT,
1950–55 THROUGH 1995–2000

Time Period	Mean Age of Initial Social Security Benefits Men	Mean Age of Initial Social Security Benefits Women	Median Age of Exit from Labor Force Men	Median Age of Exit from Labor Force Women	Mean Expected Years of Retirement Men	Mean Expected Years of Retirement Women
1950–55	68.5	67.9	66.9	67.6	12	13.6
1955–60	67.6	66.4	65.7	66.1		
1960–65	65	65	65.1	64.6		
1965–70	63.9	64.3	64.2	64.2		
1970–75	62.9	62.9	63.4	62.9		
1975–80	62.8	62.7	63	63.2		
1980–85	62.9	62.8	62.8	62.7		
1985–90	62.8	62.8	62.6	62.8	16.3	20.3
1990–95	62.7	62.6	62.4	62.3	17.2	21.3
1995–2000	62.6	62.5	62	61.4	18	22

SOURCE: Gendell 2001, tables 1 and 2.

Table 5 shows estimated mean age at initial award of Social Security benefits, and median age at exit from labor force for men and women from 1950–55 through 1995–2000. For both men and women, the average age of initial benefits decreased from the early 1950s to the early 1970s, remained fairly constant for the next two decades, and declined again in the 1990s. The age of labor force exit has generally declined over the entire period. In fact, the overall decreases since the 1970s are larger in magnitude for age of labor force exit than for age of initial benefits. This may not be surprising, given that the age of initial award of Social Security benefits cannot be lower than sixty-two.

The expected number of years of retirement is also shown in table 5 for select years. As the age of retirement has fallen, the average life expectancy has increased. Together, these two changes caused the expected number of years of retirement to increase greatly over time. From 1950–55 to 1995–2000, the expected number of years of retirement increased from 12 to 18 years for men and from 13.6 to 22 years for women. Figure 6 shows life expectancy and working-life expectancy (the number of years of life spent working) for twenty-year-old men from 1900 through 1990.

SEVEN FACTORS THAT AFFECT REDISTRIBUTION 47

FIGURE 6
MALE LIFE AND WORKING-LIFE EXPECTANCY AT AGE TWENTY, 1900-90

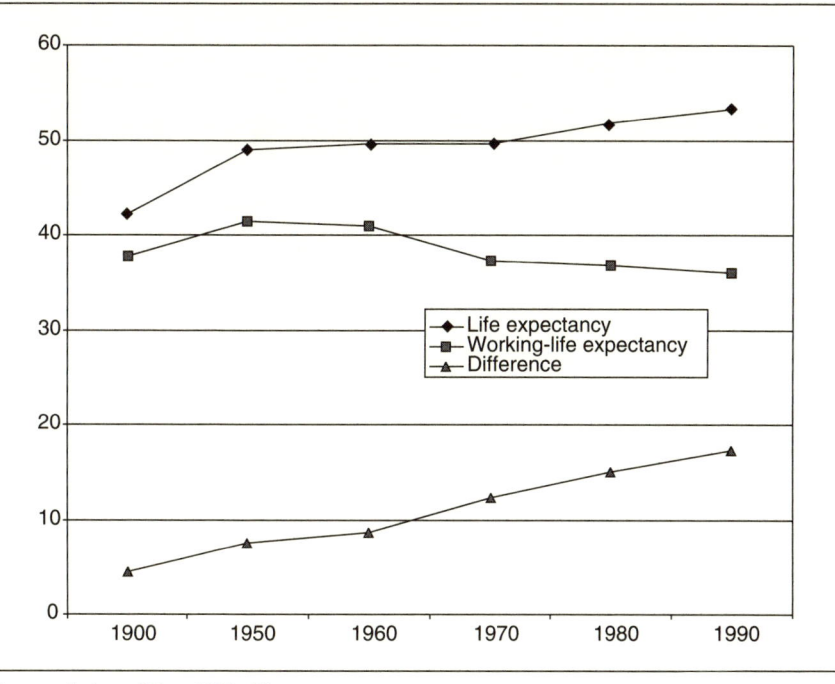

SOURCE: Stein and Foss 1999, 96.

Corresponding data for women from 1950 through 1990 are shown in figure 7. Between 1900 and 1990, life expectancy for twenty-year-old men increased eleven years, while expected working life decreased by two years. For twenty-year-old women, in contrast, both life expectancy and working-life expectancy increased by about sixteen years between 1950 and 1990. Expected working life increased overall for women despite decreasing retirement age, because of large increases in labor force participation by women at younger ages.

Retirement and Socioeconomic Status. Empirical evidence suggests retirement decisions vary with socioeconomic status. For example, Uccello (1998) examines factors influencing retirement age using the 1990 SIPP data and 1994 IRS data. He finds that men are less likely to retire if they have employer-provided health coverage. Conversely, men

48 INCOME REDISTRIBUTION FROM SOCIAL SECURITY

FIGURE 7
FEMALE LIFE AND WORKING-LIFE EXPECTANCY AT AGE TWENTY, 1950–90

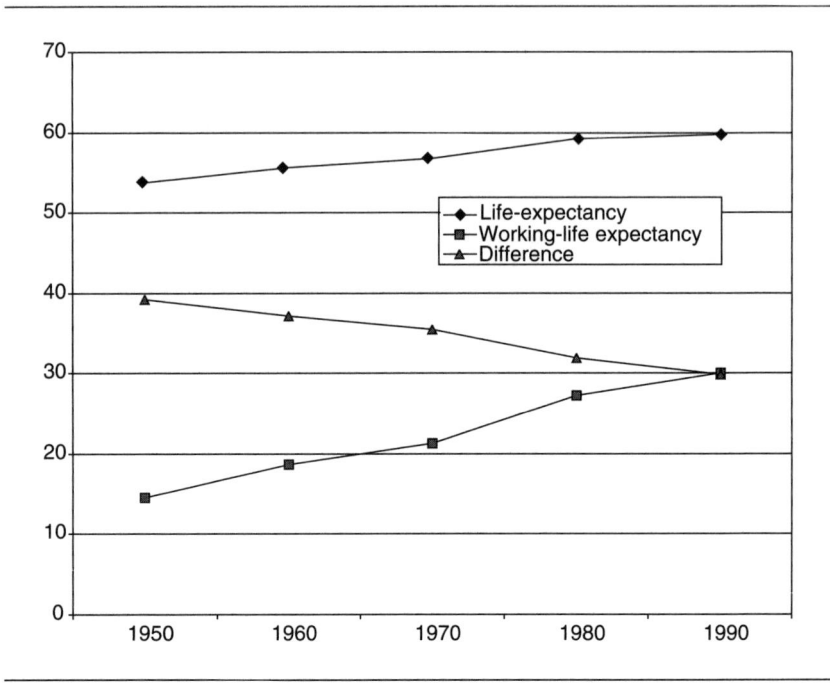

SOURCE: Stein and Foss 1999, 96.

are more likely to retire if they (1) are between the ages of sixty-one and sixty-four (compared to ages 55–60 and 65–70); (2) have multiple functional limitations; (3) work in agriculture, mining, construction, or transportation; (4) work less than twenty hours per week; (5) have pension coverage; or (6) have greater than twelve years of education.

Uccello (1998) also estimates the effect of numerous direct measures of resources on retirement. He finds that men with working spouses are less likely to retire than other men but that the probability of retiring increases with the wife's earnings. Uccello (1998) also finds that own earnings are positively related to retirement, although the effect is not statistically significantly. The effect of family wealth on men's retirement is estimated to be negative and marginally significant.

A similar analysis is performed for women. Uccello (1998) finds that women are more likely to retire if they (1) are sixty-five years old (compared to ages 55–64 and 66–70); (2) have three or more physical limitations; and (3) work in a physically demanding job. He estimates the following factors are negatively related to female retirement: (1) working between twenty and thirty-four hours per week (compared to working less than twenty hours or more than thirty-four hours per week); (2) having own employer-provided health coverage; and (3) being nonwhite.

In addition, Uccello (1998) finds female retirement is negatively related to two resource measures: presence of a working spouse and own earnings. Other studies have also found significant relationships between resources and retirement decisions. For instance, Chan and Stevens (2001) find that those with very low assets are more likely to work past age sixty-two.

Retirement and Social Security Policy. Social Security policy may also influence retirement decisions, although evidence is mixed (see Diamond and Gruber 1999 for a review). It seems likely from the retirement hazards in figure 5 that both the FRA and early retirement ages affect retirement decisions. The abrupt changes after 1961, when early retirement was introduced, suggest that many people prior to this time delayed retirement due to liquidity constraints.

Expected Social Security benefits may also influence retirement through several potential channels (such as overall generosity of benefits, changes in benefits, or benefits relative to returns from work). For instance, Gustman and Steinmeier (2002) estimate that Social Security policies delay retirement by increasing the reward for work at older ages. Stock and Wise (1990) argue that the relevant variable that may influence the retirement decision is the ratio of the return to working an additional year to the return from retirement at some future optimal date.

Diamond and Gruber (1999) analyze the effect of three retirement incentives. The first is the after-tax replacement rate, the fraction of after-tax earnings replaced by Social Security. Second, they examine the accrual rate, or the yearly percentage change in Social Security wealth. Finally, they examine the tax/subsidy rate, "the absolute change in social security wealth over the potential earnings from working that next year" (Diamond and Gruber 1999, 454). This last policy is what Stock and Wise argue is relevant. However, after reviewing the literature, Diamond and Gruber conclude

50 INCOME REDISTRIBUTION FROM SOCIAL SECURITY

that "there is only mixed evidence that changes in the overall generosity of the system has much effect on retirement behavior, although the evidence seems clearer for Social Security accrual rates than for Social Security wealth levels" (Diamond and Gruber 1999, 468).

Social Security policy can also have differential effects on retirement depending on socioeconomic status. For instance, Kahn (1988) finds a spike in retirement rates at age sixty-two for low-wealth workers, but not for very-high-wealth workers. Diamond and Gruber (1999, 461–62) find that

> before age sixty-two, there is a somewhat higher tax rate on high-wage workers since the tax/benefit linkage is reduced by the redistributive nature of benefits computation. From age sixty-two to sixty-four, there is a large subsidy to continued work for the low-earnings workers, while there is a tax on the high earners. This reflects the fact that the low-earnings workers are getting a much higher return from their social security contributions at this age. This pattern reverses from age sixty-five on, however, as the large negative accruals implicit in social security at older ages are much larger on the smaller base of earnings [for low earners]. By age sixty-nine, the implicit tax rate on low-earnings workers is over twice that on high earners.

Note, however, that Diamond and Gruber (1999) do not consider the effect of income-differentiated mortality on retirement incentives. Lower life expectancy for low earners tends to offset the incentives to work past age sixty-two caused by higher yearly returns from Social Security.

Retirement Ages in Redistribution Studies. Progressivity studies vary in their modeling of retirement age. Liebman (2002), for instance, assumes workers retire at actual retirement ages obtained from SSA records. Gustman and Steinmeier (2001) employ HRS self-reported data on expected age of retirement.[24] Other studies assume a uniform retirement age. For example, Coronado et al. (2000) assume that all workers first receive benefits at the steady-state FRA of sixty-seven (the eventual age of normal retirement after phase-in of current law). In contrast, Smith et al. (2001) estimate progressivity based on Social Security wealth at age sixty-two (the most commonly chosen age for retirement).

Assuming all workers retire at FRA is inconsistent with the fact that most workers now choose to receive Social Security benefits before they reach FRA. In 1999, for instance, 72 percent of beneficiaries received reduced benefits due to early retirement (U.S. Social Security Administration 2002c). If the net benefits from Social Security were neutral with respect to retirement age, then assuming all workers retire at the same age would make little difference in progressivity studies. And yet, as noted already, differences in life expectancy according to income lead to differences in Social Security returns for a given retirement age.

Redistribution studies also assume that Social Security policy does not influence retirement behavior. While the empirical evidence is mixed, it seems likely that retirement is at least partially determined by Social Security policy. Progressivity studies that assume otherwise may produce biased estimates of redistribution. This would be the case, for instance, if Social Security redistribution reduces work and thus replaces own income to some extent. If Social Security policy does influence retirement decisions, then this should raise concerns for studies such as Coronado et al. (2000) and Liebman (2002) that take a "steady-state" approach. Both of these studies impose current or future Social Security policies on individuals who already made choices based on earlier policies.

Cohort Analyzed

The choice of cohort used to estimate Social Security redistribution can have a large influence on the results. In this section, we examine several different factors that can cause variation among cohorts. These factors include government-imposed changes in coverage and benefits that clearly affect cohorts differently, as well as changes in socioeconomic characteristics over time.

Coverage. As discussed in chapter 2, Social Security coverage has expanded over time (see figure 1). At the inception of Social Security, the program covered only about half the workforce. Today, 96 percent of workers pay Social Security taxes.

Due to the expansion in Social Security coverage over time, progressivity estimates for older cohorts with less coverage might differ substantially from estimates for younger cohorts. Social Security Administration earnings data include information only for those workers covered by the program. Use of these data can affect estimates of progressivity in two ways. First, individuals in uncovered occupations, such as domestic services, tend to have low income; and they are not included in any measure of redistribution. If Social Security appears to redistribute toward the bottom of the income distribution but does not redistribute toward even-poorer individuals excluded from the data, then Social Security may appear to be more progressive than it truly is. Second, even if we limit the income distribution to those observed in SSA records, progressivity estimates still cannot account for the earnings of individuals during certain years of uncovered employment.

Among recent micro simulation studies, Liebman's (2002) 1925–39 cohort is the oldest (comparing Bosworth et al. 1999; Caldwell et al. 1999; Coronado et al. 2000; Gustman and Steinmeier 2001; Smith et al. 2001; and Liebman 2002). Many people in Liebman's cohort, taken from SSA earnings records, would likely have worked in noncovered employment at some point. To address this possibility, he deletes government employees and retirees. Even in this new subsample, half the primary earners in the lowest income quintile had fewer than thirty-five years of covered employment, compared to 22 percent in the second quintile, 13 percent in the third quintile, and less than 2 percent in the fourth and fifth quintiles. Liebman (2002, 30) notes that "many of the non-immigrants in this first quintile are likely to have worked in noncovered sectors of the economy, and therefore their years with zero earnings are not true zeros. Thus, an argument could be made for ignoring the results for the lowest-income quintile and focusing on the remaining four quintiles."

Of course, it is also possible for a person to work a substantial number of years in noncovered employment and still have thirty-five or more years of covered employment. As discussed in chapter 2, only the highest thirty-five years of covered earnings are used to determine Social Security benefits. In addition, earnings tend to increase with experience (at least initially). Hence, workers switching from uncovered to covered employment may pay lower lifetime taxes, with little or no offsetting reduction in benefits. Therefore, beneficiaries who spend relatively less time in covered employment could receive large net transfers from workers who spend relatively more time in covered employment.

In addition to being uncovered prior to 1950, self-employed workers also faced lower Social Security tax rates from 1951 through 1983 than wage and salary workers. This also tends to increase net transfers to workers switching from noncovered to covered employment. Transfers based on the amount of covered employment are an aspect of redistribution that has been largely neglected in recent micro simulation studies (Gustman and Steinmeier's 2000 study comparing Social Security's treatment of natives and immigrants is a noteworthy exception).

The direction of bias on progressivity estimates caused by workers switching from uncovered to covered employment is not obvious. Since Social Security's inception, coverage has been extended to include many high-income workers, such as the self-employed and professionals (doctors and lawyers). Yet coverage also expanded to include relatively low-income workers, such as government employees. To our knowledge, no estimates exist of the overall income distribution of workers switching from uncovered to covered employment.

Net Benefits. In addition to expanding coverage, the government has increased benefits and changed tax rates over time. Early recipients of Social Security benefits received large net transfers. More recent cohorts, however, can expect to receive much smaller net transfers from Social Security on average, relative to older cohorts. Leimer (1995), for instance, estimates that the 1876 birth cohort received an internal rate of return of 36.5 percent on their Social Security tax payments. The 1975 birth cohort, on the other hand, will receive a 1.7 percent internal rate of return. Caldwell et al. (1999) and Smith et al. (2001) also estimate that Social Security taxes have increased relative to benefits for later cohorts.

One might argue that the redistribution across cohorts should not necessarily affect estimates of within-cohort redistribution. It does mean, however, that the amount of redistribution within earlier cohorts is likely to be different from the amount of redistribution within later cohorts.

Therefore, the choice of cohort becomes important, as it can affect the estimate of within-cohort redistribution. Recent studies try to compensate for this variation by focusing on the steady state. For instance, Coronado et al. (2000, 1) select a "future" cohort by choosing to "take a steady state approach in which all working and retirement years come under the current system. We thus focus on intra-generational redistribution and ignore effects between age cohorts. In this sense we assess the long-run effects of the current system." To abstract from the age of their sample, Coronado et al. (2000) adjust earnings for real wage growth.

Liebman (2002, 13) takes a similar approach:

> In order for my results to reflect the U.S. Social Security system in a steady state rather than one in which the rates of return earned by different cohorts are changing, and to make the results comparable to studies that focus on Social Security reforms that would be implemented over the coming century, I calibrate the life expectancies and payroll tax rates to reflect conditions in 2075, the endpoint of the Social Security actuaries' 75-year horizon.

To simulate conditions in 2075, Liebman scales his mortality estimates to those born in 1990 and assumes a 15.4 percent tax rate (as is necessary to pay the steady-state benefits).

Social Security Policy, SES, and Progressivity. Studies that estimate steady-state redistribution implicitly assume that within-cohort transfers are independent of the age of the cohort. However, this assumption may not be appropriate if changes in Social Security policy over time have had differential effects according to SES. For instance, the change to allow early retirement reduced the mortality penalty for lower earners and thus made Social Security more progressive. Similarly, increases over time in the amount of income subject to the tax relative to average wages likely increased within-cohort progressivity as well.

In addition to changes in Social Security policy, two major changes in the socioeconomic composition of society have affected within-cohort progressivity: labor force participation and marital status. Labor force participation for men has fallen since Social Security's enactment, in large part due to the decreased participation of older men, while female labor force participation has increased significantly over this time. Specifically, women made up 28.5 percent of the workforce in 1948, compared to 46.2 percent in 1998. Marital status also has changed significantly since Social Security's enactment. In 1971, 4 percent of women aged eighteen and older in the United States were divorced; by 1998, this percentage had increased to 10.8. And, "Social Security is anything but neutral with respect to marital status" (Caldwell et al. 1999, 117).

Spousal and survivor benefits are not received by single women, divorced women who were married for less than ten years, and married women who earn more income than their spouse. Thus, the increases in female labor force participation and divorce rates have both served to reduce spouse and survivor benefits relative to total benefits. For the 1931–35 birth cohorts, Smith et al. (2001) estimate that 24.5 percent of all Social Security benefits are spouse and survivor benefits. Conversely, they find that these auxiliary benefits will constitute only 13.1 percent of total benefits for those born between 1956 and 1960.

Smith et al. (2001) note that economic and demographic trends have tended to increase the amount of redistribution over time. In particular, they find that spousal and survivor benefits interacted with marital histories increased progressivity over time: "Among more recent cohorts, the reduced importance of auxiliary benefits (due to higher lifetime earnings of women) and the increase in the proportion of retirees who are divorced makes [Social Security] more progressive than for cohorts who retired in the 1990's, even as the net benefit . . . declines" (Smith et al. 2001, 18). Steuerle and Bakija (1994) also find that Social Security has become more progressive as cohort rates of return have fallen.

If Steuerle and Bakija (1994) and Smith et al. (2001) are correct, then estimates of progressivity for older cohorts may not accurately reflect the current or future progressivity of Social Security. Liebman (2002) examines a 1925–29 birth cohort. Gustman and Steinmeier (2001) analyze data for a cohort born between 1931 and 1941. Coronado et al.'s (2000) sample includes some relatively younger workers: 25 percent of their sample is under thirty between 1968 and 1989. Of these three, Coronado et al.'s results should be the most progressive (since their sample is the youngest). However, they include only individuals whose relationship to head of household did not change during the sample period. Therefore, their sample selection criteria disproportionately eliminate women, specifically women with changes in marital status. By eliminating divorced women from their sample, Coronado et al. (2000) may underestimate progressivity by ignoring "a potentially rich form of social security benefit variation" (Caldwell et al. 1999, 117).

While some studies have attempted to adjust for some cohort-specific factors affecting redistribution (such as mortality, real wage growth, and tax rates), it is unlikely that a study could control for all cohort-specific factors affecting progressivity. For instance, while Liebman (2002) applies future mortality and payroll tax rates to his 1925–29 cohort, he does not control for changes in labor force participation and marital status.

Studies such as Liebman (2002) and Coronado et al. (2000) that apply current or future Social Security policy to older cohorts also assume that behavior such as earnings patterns and retirement are not affected by changes in Social Security policy. And yet, evidence indicates behavior is affected by Social Security (Gruber and Wise 1999; Diamond and Gruber 1999; Chan and Stevens 2001; Dominitz et al. 2002).

Due to this potential endogeneity, one could argue that the approach of Gustman and Steinmeier (2001) regarding cohort-specific effects has an advantage over that of Coronado et al. (2000) and Liebman (2002). Their "analysis uses the current benefit and the tax schedules in place at the time wages were earned" (Gustman and Steinmeier 2001, 8). They acknowledge that their estimates are cohort specific and thus may not accurately reflect current or future redistribution. However, they also do not introduce potential bias by adjusting only partially for cohort-specific effects.

Behavioral Effects

"David Friedman's Second Law" states that "the government cannot give anything away" (Friedman 1996, 295). This statement refers to the tendency of government transfer programs to change behavior in ways that mitigate the benefits of those very same transfer programs. Progressivity studies assume (at least implicitly) that redistribution does not affect behavior. Of course, it is possible that redistribution from Social Security affects behavior in a variety of ways. If so, then existing progressivity estimates that assume no change in behavior may be biased.[25]

Earnings. Redistribution may influence earnings behavior. If the rate of return on Social Security taxes is equal to the rate of return from investing those same funds, then earnings behavior might not be affected by Social Security (Feldstein and Liebman 2002c). However, that scenario involves no redistribution. In reality, Social Security involves redistribution that changes rates of return, both across and within cohorts. Therefore, one might expect Social Security to influence earnings.

Social Security could have an effect on earnings by changing work incentives. Feldstein and Samwick (1992) find that Social Security tax rates vary greatly with demographics. They find that women and young workers often receive no extra benefits from paying Social Security payroll taxes, a zero rate of return on those "contributions." Women might not benefit from paying Social Security taxes because they often end up receiving spousal or survivor benefits based solely on their husbands' earnings. Also, young people might not benefit if they are not yet in their highest thirty-five years of earnings. Feldstein and Samwick (1992) note that a married man close to retirement who has a low-earning spouse could face a negative net tax rate (additional benefits that exceed the additional taxes), since he likely is in his highest earnings years and has a wife who will also receive benefits based on his taxes. Such individuals may therefore be induced to work harder, earn more, and end up in a higher-income category, so that the redistribution toward them makes the system look less progressive.

Of course, Social Security net tax rates vary according to income, where the amount of variation depends on how income is measured. For instance, net tax rates on lifetime income vary less than rates on annual income. Even for a given measure of lifetime income, net tax rates also vary due to differences between cohorts in labor force participation and marital patterns. Rates on household income vary less than rates on individual income, and rates on potential income vary less than rates on actual income. Thus, measures of relative redistribution are generally smaller in

58 INCOME REDISTRIBUTION FROM SOCIAL SECURITY

studies that use a more inclusive measure of income to classify people from rich to poor.

The degree to which Social Security net taxes influence earnings depends on the responsiveness of labor supply to changes in the net wage. In general, it is estimated that primary earners are rather insensitive to changes in wages, while secondary earners are fairly responsive to changes in wages (Eissa and Hoynes 1996). To understand how this can affect measures of progressivity, consider the following example. Suppose women have larger labor supply elasticities and large net Social Security benefits that induce them to work less, ending up in a lower income category. Then, redistribution toward them makes Social Security look more progressive.

Social Security transfers can also affect the labor supply decisions of beneficiaries. Specifically, Friedberg (2000) estimates the labor supply effects of the Social Security earnings test. She finds that workers respond to the earnings test by "bunching" just below the exempt amount and that "the clustering moves when the [exempt amount] moves, and disappears when the earnings test is eliminated. The clustering is evidence that the earnings test leads some beneficiaries to hold down their labor supply" (Friedberg 2000, 61). Thus, beneficiaries may provide less labor than their optimal amount, earn less income, and cause Social Security to be more progressive.

Retirement Age. As discussed earlier in this chapter (see pages 49–50), Social Security might also influence decisions to enter or exit the labor force (see Diamond and Gruber 1999 for a review). The fact that people tend to retire when first eligible for Social Security benefits suggests retirement is strongly related to Social Security eligibility (see table 5 and figure 5). In addition to eligibility, expected Social Security payments may also influence retirement decisions (Diamond and Gruber 1999; Gustman and Steinmeier 2002).

Retirement incentives created by Social Security can vary with respect to socioeconomic status. Diamond and Gruber (1999) find that Social Security provides incentives for very low earners to stay in the labor force from ages sixty-two to sixty-four, while the opposite is true for very high earners. Kahn (1988) provides conflicting evidence; he reports that low-wealth workers increase retirement at age sixty-two, while very-high-wealth workers do not.

If low-wealth workers retire earlier and get placed into a lower lifetime earnings category, then redistribution toward them looks more progressive. With potential income, however, the low-wealth early retiree gets placed into the same lifetime earnings category as if he had continued working, and Social Security looks less progressive. Avoiding these behavioral benefits is part of the *point* of using "potential income" rather than actual income (see pages 35–37 in this chapter).

Social Security might also influence retirement by changing "social conventions regarding retirement dates, affecting the design of private pension plans, firm mandatory retirement ages (no longer legal in the United States), and worker tastes" (Feldstein and Liebman 2002b, 2282). Indeed, when attempting to explain why retirement rates are so high at age sixty-five, Lumsdaine et al. (1995, 27) "are inclined to attribute the unexplained high age 65 departure rates to an 'age 65 effect', that is, to the influence of custom or accepted practice."

Savings. Statistics are often touted regarding the percentage of elderly kept out of poverty by Social Security. For example, figure 8 presents SSA estimates of the percentage of beneficiaries who lived in poverty in 1999, as well as the percent who would have lived in poverty had they not received Social Security. The SSA reports that 48 percent of beneficiaries would be in poverty without Social Security, compared to only 8 percent with Social Security. For blacks, 61 percent would be in poverty without Social Security, compared to 21 percent with Social Security.

The estimates in figure 8 assume that Social Security does not affect savings. Yet, theory and empirical evidence suggest that private saving *is* reduced by Social Security. In fact, an actuarially fair program would be expected to reduce private savings in equal proportion to Social Security benefits (Feldstein and Liebman 2002b, 2275). As noted previously, redistribution results in variation in rates of return from Social Security across income groups. In general, those receiving net transfers from Social Security tend to save less than those paying net taxes, other things equal. Therefore, any redistribution built into the system tends to be offset by

60 INCOME REDISTRIBUTION FROM SOCIAL SECURITY

FIGURE 8
POVERTY AMONG SOCIAL SECURITY BENEFICIARIES, 1999

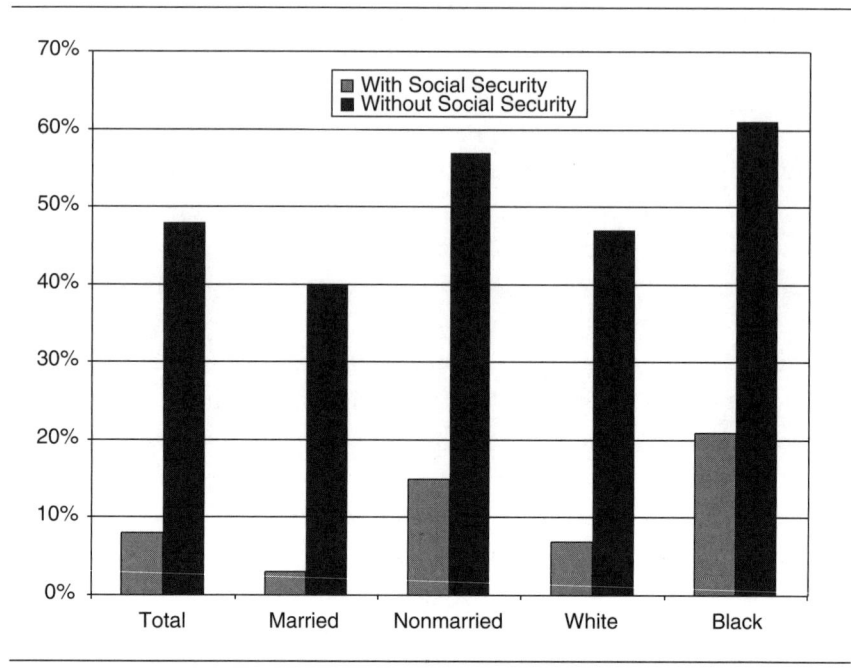

SOURCE: U.S. Social Security Administration 2002c, slide 5.

reductions in savings by those who expect to receive net transfers on retirement.

Estimates of the actual effect of Social Security on savings vary. A Congressional Budget Office review concluded that "each dollar of Social Security wealth most likely reduces private wealth by between zero and 50 cents, with the most likely estimate lying near the middle of that range" (Congressional Budget Office 1998, 17). This implies that a substantial portion of redistributed Social Security benefits have no effect on poverty among the elderly.

Resources Devoted to Obtaining Net Transfers. Considerable resources are spent to influence Social Security policy. For example, the AARP is committed to preserving Social Security. They had total revenue of $595 million in 2001, of which $57 million went toward "legislation, research, and development" (AARP 2002, 12). This figure is likely a lower bound for their actual resources devoted to advocacy. For instance, they spent $152 million on publications, which also promote their policy positions. In addition, other organizations devote resources to reduce Social Security redistribution.

Economists refer to *rent* as payment above what is necessary to induce supply for a particular good or service. An example of a rent is anybody's Social Security benefit above what would be received if benefits were proportional to taxes paid. *Rent seeking* is a term economists use to describe attempts to obtain rents. Likewise, *rent avoidance* refers to attempts to prevent resources from being transferred. Both rent seeking and rent avoidance include political activities such as writing letters to the editor and legislators, canvassing, and lobbying.

Both rent seeking and rent avoidance are socially wasteful in the sense that they argue over how to divide existing resources and create no new value. In fact, they use up resources that have alternative *productive* uses (Tullock 1967). For example, a car thief's time is socially wasted because no value is created by theft.[26] Time spent stealing cars has more productive uses (working in an auto factory, for instance), and resources devoted to avoiding theft also have alternative uses that are more socially productive. Similarly, while resources used up trying to influence returns from Social Security generate personal benefits, they do so only at the expense of others. Resources devoted to influencing net transfers via Social Security could also be used in alternative ways that make society better off.

Certainly, resources devoted to obtaining net transfers from Social Security offset some of the potential social benefits from redistribution. The magnitude of this loss is uncertain, however.

General Equilibrium Effects. Gains from Social Security redistribution may be reduced by price changes. To quote Feldstein and Liebman, (2002b, 2289–90):

> A Social Security system that alters saving and labor supply behavior will generally change the total amount of capital and labor supplied in the economy. These changes in factor supplies will alter wages and the returns to capital. These changes

can be important because individual responses to the changing factor prices can offset some of the direct impact of government policies, because these price changes alter the distribution of income between workers and owners of capital, and because the optimal policy response to population aging is sensitive to how the demographic changes alter the relative supplies of capital and labor.

In addition to changes in the relative prices of labor and capital, prices of other goods in the economy can also change in response to government transfers. For instance, Susin (2002) examines the effect of rent vouchers on low-income housing prices. He estimates that, on average, rent vouchers have increased rents in large metro areas by 16 percent, "a large effect consistent with a low supply elasticity in the low quality rental housing market. Considered as a transfer program, this result implies that vouchers have caused a $8.2 billion increase in the total rent paid by low-income non-recipients, while only providing a subsidy of $5.8 billion to recipients, resulting in a net loss of $2.4 billion to low-income households" (Susin 2002, 109).

Dee (2000) provides further evidence of "Friedman's Second Law." He estimates that much of the benefits to poor school districts from state school finance equalization plans are offset by increases in housing costs. More money for schools might increase land and house prices, which is a *capitalization effect*. Likewise, changes in relative prices may mitigate the potential benefits from Social Security redistribution. This might occur because demand for goods and services tends to vary with income. For example, as is the case for rent vouchers (Susin 2002), Social Security redistribution toward low-income people might be partially offset by increases in housing prices in low-income areas. Net transfers to women could be mitigated by increases in the relative prices of goods and services consumed largely by women, such as women's apparel.

Uncertainty. While current Social Security policy can influence current behavior, uncertainty regarding future Social Security policy may also affect today's decisions. Social Security cannot remain solvent in the future without significant benefit cuts or tax increases. Risk regarding future policy changes might influence numerous behaviors, particularly the savings behavior of current workers, who feel uncertain about the future existence of Social Security. Suppose they save more because of this uncertainty, and this extra savings reduces the market rate of return on savings. The uncertainty then tends to injure those most risk averse and therefore provides relative gains to those least risk averse. If those two types of people are not uniformly distributed across the income distribution, then policy uncertainty about Social Security can affect the system's progressivity.

5

Conclusions

Social Security's progressive benefit schedule has led many to believe the program transfers money from the rich to the poor. However, many other factors can influence the empirical calculations of Social Security redistribution. Studies performed by Coronado et al. (1999, 2000, 2002), Gustman and Steinmeier (2001), Liebman (2002), and Feldstein and Liebman (2002c) take these factors into consideration and find that Social Security is, at least, not very progressive and might in fact be regressive—transferring money from the poor to the rich!

We show that the assumptions the researcher makes to perform the analysis of Social Security redistribution can influence the results. All the measures of redistribution in the literature require calculations of Social Security taxes paid and benefits received for every individual. Thus, any empirical measure of redistribution is a function of the variables used to determine net Social Security transfers.

First, we discussed the importance of mortality estimates. Since Social Security is a defined-benefit annuity, longevity is crucial to the amount of benefit received. Therefore, to have an accurate estimate of benefits received by each worker, we must first make an assumption about his mortality. All the studies reviewed here that incorporate SES-differentiated mortality estimates find that Social Security appears less progressive.

Another key variable that can affect the estimate of redistribution via calculations of net Social Security transfers is income. Numerous methods are utilized to measure income. The traditional classification of individuals by annual income leads to progressive outcomes, whereas a switch to lifetime income makes it less progressive. This is primarily because the annual measure is a snapshot view that may classify elderly and young individuals with high lifetime income as poor.

CONCLUSIONS 65

Those who are able to use total earnings find that Social Security is less progressive than those who are limited by their data to earnings below the cap. Use of potential income, as opposed to actual income, also causes redistribution to appear less progressive, since this measure of income assigns earnings to nonworking spouses and other workers who do not have thirty-five years of earnings. Similarly, assigning each individual a share of household income has the same effect. We note that the existing literature measures gross income, before any taxes and transfers occur. To our knowledge, no redistribution studies have considered income net of taxes and transfers. Due to data limitations, no adjustments for cost of living across geographic localities are made in the literature. This could also affect progressivity estimates, although the direction is unclear.

In the next section, we discussed the decision to exclude workers not covered by Social Security. These workers could include the self-employed prior to 1950, civilian employees of the federal government hired before 1984, and workers of the underground economy. Social Security benefits are based on the highest thirty-five years of covered employment. Therefore, workers who spend less time in covered employment could receive transfers from those spending more time in such employment. To our knowledge, no researchers have calculated redistribution either between covered and uncovered employment or between self-employed and wage and salary workers.

The choice of the discount rate is yet another decision that influences calculations of net transfers and estimates of redistribution. We know that the Social Security tax is regressive, while the benefit schedule is designed to be progressive. In general, the greater the discount rate, the more weight is placed on the taxation portion of Social Security and the less progressive is the overall system. All studies reviewed find that higher discount rates cause the Social Security system to appear less progressive and maybe even regressive.

Next, we examined the researcher's choice of retirement age for the sample, as well as the choice of cohort analyzed. For the former, assuming a uniform retirement age should not matter as long as early benefits are actuarially fair and mortality estimates are income differentiated. The choice of cohort to analyze can be important for a couple of reasons. Each cohort experienced changes in government policies about covered employment and net tax rates at different points in their working lives. These changes affected each cohort differently, and estimates of within-cohort redistribution varied for different cohorts. Both Coronado et al. (2000) and Liebman (2002) try to compensate for this by focusing on the steady state.

In the final section, we mentioned several decisions made by individuals that could be influenced by Social Security policy. For instance, expected benefit levels could affect decisions about labor force participation, age of retirement, and savings. Due to this potential endogeneity, studies that assume Social Security policy does not influence individual behavior may be biased.

Clearly, the many assumptions and measurement decisions about individuals and data that are necessary to analyze the redistribution from Social Security can affect the outcome. To summarize, the following choices all cause Social Security to appear less progressive than otherwise:

1. Mortality estimates differentiated by income or education, rather than uniform.

2. Lifetime income, rather than annual income.

3. Total earnings, rather than those below the earnings cap.

4. Potential income, rather than actual income.

5. Household income, rather than individual income.

6. Higher discount rates, rather than lower ones.

Notes

1. The tax rates in table 1 are for the OASDI program, which we refer to as Social Security in this study.

2. Specifically, the "formula states that the base for any year Y after 1994 is equal to the 1994 base of $60,600 multiplied by the ratio of the national average wage index for year (Y − 2) to that for 1992, with the result rounded to the nearest multiple of $300. If the result is less than the current base, the base is *not* reduced" (U.S. Social Security Administration 2002b).

3. The monthly reductions for early retirement are $5/_9$ of a percent for the first thirty-six months and $5/_{12}$ of a percent for additional months.

4. This section draws heavily on Diamond and Gruber (1999).

5. For example, if AIME were $4,000 in 2003, the PIA would be calculated as PIA = 0.90(606) + 0.32(3653 − 606) + 0.15(4000 − 3653) = 1572.49.

6. Low earnings are defined as 45 percent of the Social Security average wage index. Medium earnings equal the average wage index, and high earnings equal taxable maximum earnings (Committee on Ways and Means 2000, 57, table 1-7).

7. See, for instance, Hurd and Shoven (1985); Boskin et al. (1987); Steuerle and Bakija (1994); Panis and Lillard (1996); and Diamond and Gruber (1999). This section draws heavily on Caldwell et al. (1999).

8. Hurd et al. (2001) analyze data from Asset and Health Dynamics of the Oldest Old (AHEAD), a panel survey of individuals born prior to 1924 and their spouses. They find that the relationship between mortality and SES in the AHEAD data decreases with age. This may be due to sample selection, however. "Because the AHEAD survey . . . excludes the institutionalized population, as age increases, members of the survey become progressively more healthy in comparison to the overall population. . . . Thus, one should be careful in making statements such as 'the mortality gradient, whether a function of wealth, income, or education, apparently decreases with age'" (Welsh 2001, 198).

9. Of course, determining causality among income, risk factors correlated with income, and mortality can be problematic. Unmeasured personal characteristics (such as genetic predispositions) could lead to risk factors (such as obesity), low earnings, and decreased life expectancy.

10. Kenkel (1991), for instance, finds that the effects of education on smoking persist after controlling for family income and for knowledge of smoking risks.

11. Age-adjusted death rates are adjusted to "eliminate the effects of differences in the age composition from comparisons among populations" (Keppel et al. 2002, 13).

12. Some studies have found that black mortality rates fall below those of whites at older ages (see Sorlie et al. 1992, for instance). Others contend that this "crossover" effect is an artifact of data errors (Preston et al. 1996). Brown (2002) finds little crossover evidence in the National Longitudinal Mortality Study data.

13. This section draws heavily on Brown (2002).

14. This sections draws heavily on Allegretto and Arthur (2001).

15. Smith et al. (2001) control for life-expectancy variation due to single or married status. They do not differentiate singles between those never married, divorced, or widowed.

16. Slight variations of mortality estimates by Brown et al. (2002) are used by Liebman (2002), Brown (2002), and Feldstein and Liebman (2002c). For instance, Brown (2002) differentiates mortality according to ethnicity, race, and education, while Liebman (2002) does not adjust mortality for ethnic variation.

17. See note 15.

18. This section draws heavily on Caldwell et al. (1999).

19. Diamond and Gruber's 1999 retirement age study does simulate whether Social Security benefits are subject to taxation.

20. The price index for College Station is 86, compared to 136.9 for Boston. Cost-of-living adjustments are based on ACCRA 4th quarter 1999 data (http://www.accra.org).

21. As elsewhere, we assume that the worker incurs the total cost of taxes on the worker and employer.

22. This section draws heavily on Caldwell et al. (1999).

23. Here we use the Social Security Administration's definition of *retirement*, meaning the age at which Social Security benefits are first claimed. As discussed in chapter 2, however, a person does not have to withdraw from the labor force to receive benefits.

24. Gustman and Steinmeier (2001) assume retirement at age sixty-two for those with no self-reported expected retirement age. They assume retirement at age seventy for those reporting expected retirement ages beyond seventy, or those reporting that they never expect to retire (see Gustman and Steinmeier 2001, 15, footnote 17).

25. This section draws heavily on Feldstein and Liebman (2002b).

26. The analogy between the social cost of theft and rent seeking was first made by Tullock (1967).

References

AARP. 2002. http://www.aarp.org/ar/2001/graphics/ar_2001.pdf (accessed December 16, 2002).
Allegretto, Sylvia A., and Michelle M. Arthur. 2001. An Empirical Analysis of Homosexual/Heterosexual Male Earnings Differentials: Unmarried and Unequal? *Industrial and Labor Relations Review* 54, no. 3 (April): 631–46.
Badgett, M. V. Lee. 1995. The Wage Effects of Sexual Orientation Discrimination. *Industrial and Labor Relations Review* 48, no. 4 (July): 726–39.
———. 1997. Beyond Biased Samples: Challenging the Myths on the Economic Status of Lesbians and Gay Men. In *Homo Economics*, ed. Amy Gluckman and Betsy Reed, 65–72. New York and London: Routledge.
———. 1998. Income Inflation: The Myth of Affluence among Gay, Lesbian, and Bisexual Americans. Report of the Institute for Gay and Lesbian Strategic Studies. http://www.iglss.org/media/files/income.pdf.
———. 2001. *Money, Myths, and Change: The Economic Lives of Lesbians and Gay Men*. Chicago: University of Chicago Press.
Badgett, M. V. Lee, C. Donnelly, and J. Kibbe. 1992. Pervasive Patterns of Discrimination against Lesbians and Gay Men. Report of the National Gay and Lesbian Task Force Policy Institute.
Boskin, Michael J., Laurence J. Kotlikoff, Douglas J. Puffert, and John B. Shoven. 1987. Social Security: A Financial Appraisal across and within Generations. *National Tax Journal* 40, no. 1:19–34.
Bosworth, Barry, Gary Burtless, and Eugene Steuerle. 1999. Lifetime Earnings Patterns, the Distribution of Future Social Security Benefits, and the Impact of Pension Reform. Center for Retirement Research at Boston College (December).
Broadus, Joseph E. 1994. Employment Nondiscrimination Act of 1994: Hearing on S. 2238 before the Senate Committee on Labor and Human Resources. 103rd Congress. July 29.
Brown, Jeffrey R. 2002. Differential Mortality and the Value of Individual Account Retirement Annuities. In *The Distributional Aspects of Social Security and Social Security Reform*, ed. Martin Feldstein and Jeffrey B. Liebman, 401–46. Chicago: University of Chicago Press for NBER.

Brown, Jeffrey R., Jeffrey B. Liebman, and Joshua Pollet. 2002. Appendix: Estimating Life Tables That Reflect Socioeconomic Differences in Mortality. In *The Distributional Aspects of Social Security and Social Security Reform*, ed. Martin Feldstein and Jeffrey B. Liebman, 447–57. Chicago: University of Chicago Press for NBER.

Burtless, Gary, and Robert Moffitt. 1984. The Effect of Social Security Benefits on the Labor Supply of the Aged. In *Retirement and Economic Behavior*, ed. Henry Aaron and Gary Burtless. Washington, D.C.: Brookings Institution Press.

Caldwell, Steven et al. 1999. Social Security's Treatment of Postwar Americans. In *Tax Policy and the Economy* 13, ed. James Poterba, 109–48. Cambridge, Mass.: The MIT Press for NBER.

Chan, Sewin, and Ann Huff Stevens. 2001. Retirement Incentives and Expectations. NBER working paper 8082. National Bureau of Economic Research, Cambridge, Mass. (January).

Committee on Ways and Means, U.S. House of Representatives. 2000. *2000 Green Book: Background Material and Data on Programs within the Jurisdiction of the Committee on Ways and Means*. Washington, D.C.: U.S. Government Printing Office. October 6.

Congressional Budget Office. 1998. *Social Security and Private Saving: A Review of the Empirical Evidence*. Washington D.C.: U.S. Government Printing Office.

Coronado, Julia Lynn, Don Fullerton, and Thomas Glass. 1999. Distributional Impacts of Proposed Changes to the Social Security System. In *Tax Policy and the Economy* 13, ed. James Poterba. Cambridge, Mass.: The MIT Press for NBER.

———. 2000. The Progressivity of Social Security. NBER working paper 7520. National Bureau of Economic Research, Cambridge, Mass. (February).

———. 2002. Long-Run Effects of Social Security Reform Proposals on Lifetime Progressivity. In *The Distributional Aspects of Social Security and Social Security Reform*, ed. Martin Feldstein and Jeffrey B. Liebman, 149–205. Chicago: University of Chicago Press for NBER.

Deaton, Angus. 2001. The Policy Implications of the Gradiant. Center for Health and Wellbeing working paper. Princeton University, Princeton, N.J. (September).

Deaton, Angus, and Christina Paxson. 1999. Mortality, Education, Income, and Inequality among American Cohorts. NBER working paper 7140. National Bureau of Economic Research, Cambridge, Mass. (May).

———. 2001. Mortality, Income, and Income Inequality over Time in Britain and the United States. NBER working paper 8534. National Bureau of Economic Research, Cambridge, Mass. (October).

Dee, Thomas. 2000. The Capitalization of Education Finance Reforms. *Journal of Law and Economics* 43, no. 1 (April): 185–214.

Diamond, Peter, and Jonathan Gruber. 1999. Social Security and Retirement in the U.S. In *Social Security and Retirement around the World*, ed. Jonathan Gruber and David A. Wise, 437–74. Chicago: University of Chicago Press for NBER.

REFERENCES

Dominitz, Jeff, Charles F. Manski, and Jordan Heinz. 2002. Social Security Expectations and Retirement Savings Decisions. NBER working paper 8718. National Bureau of Economic Research, Cambridge, Mass.

Duleep, H. 1989. Measuring Socioeconomic Mortality Differences over Time. *Demography* 26 (May): 345–51.

Dumond, J. Michael, Barry T. Hirsch, and David A. Macpherson. 1999. Wage Differentials across Labor Markets and Workers: Does Cost of Living Matter? *Economic Inquiry* 37, no. 4 (October): 577–98.

Eissa, Nada, and Hilary Williamson Hoynes. 1996. Labor Supply Response to the Earned Income Tax Credit. *Quarterly Journal of Economics* 111, no. 2 (May): 605–37.

Feinstein, J. S. 1993. The Relationship between Socioeconomic Status and Health: A Review of the Literature. *Milbank Quarterly* 71, no. 2:279–322.

Feldstein, Martin, and Jeffrey B. Liebman, eds. 2002a. *Distributional Aspects of Social Security and Social Security Reform*. Chicago: University of Chicago Press for NBER.

———. 2002b. Social Security. In *Handbook of Public Economics* 4, ed. Alan J. Auerbach and Martin Feldstein, 2245–2324. Amsterdam: North-Holland.

———. 2002c. The Distributional Effects of an Investment-Based Social Security System. In *The Distributional Aspects of Social Security and Social Security Reform*, ed. Martin Feldstein and Jeffrey B. Liebman, 263–326. Chicago: University of Chicago Press for NBER.

Feldstein, Martin, and A. Samwick. 1992. Social Security Rules and Marginal Tax Rates. *National Tax Journal* 45:1–22.

Friedberg, Leora. 2000. The Labor Supply Effects of the Social Security Earnings Test. *Review of Economics and Statistics* 82, no.1 (February): 48–63.

Friedman, David. 1996. *Hidden Order: The Economics of Everyday Life*. New York: HarperCollins.

Fuchs, Victor R., Mark McClellan, and Jonathan Skinner. 2001. Area Differences in Utilization of Medical Care and Mortality among U.S. Elderly. NBER working paper 8628. National Bureau of Economic Research, Cambridge, Mass. (December).

Gendell, Murray. 2001. Retirement Age Declines Again in the 1990s. *Bureau of Labor Statistics Monthly Labor Review* (October): 12–21.

Gruber, Jonathan, and David A. Wise. 1999. Introduction and Summary. In *Social Security and Retirement around the World*, ed. Jonathan Gruber and David A. Wise, 1–35. Chicago: University of Chicago Press for NBER.

Gustman, Alan L., and Thomas L. Steinmeier. 2000. Social Security Benefits of Immigrants and U.S. Born. In *Issues in the Economics of Immigration*, ed. George J. Borjas, 309–50. Chicago: University of Chicago Press for NBER.

———. 2001. How Effective Is Redistribution under the Social Security Benefit Formula? *Journal of Public Economics* 82:1–28.

———. 2002. Social Security, Pensions and Retirement Behavior within the Family. NBER working paper 8772. National Bureau of Economic Research, Cambridge, Mass. (February).

Hamermesh, Daniel S., and Albert Rees. 1993. *The Economics of Work and Pay*. New York: Harper Collins College Publishers.

Hewitt, Christopher. 1995. The Socioeconomic Position of Gay Men: A Review of the Evidence. *American Journal of Economics and Sociology* 54, no. 4 (October): 461–79.

Hogg, R. S., S. A. Strathdee, K. J. Craib, M. V. O'Shaughnessy, J. S. Montaner, and M. T. Schechter. 1997. Modelling the Impact of HIV Disease on Mortality in Gay and Bisexual Men. *International Journal of Epidemiology* 26:657–61.

Hurd, Michael D., Daniel McFadden, and Angela Merrill. 2001. Predictors of Mortality among the Elderly. In *Themes in the Economics of Aging*, ed. David Wise, 171–97. Chicago: University of Chicago Press for NBER.

Hurd, Michael D., and John B. Shoven. 1985. The Distributional Impact of Social Security. In *Pensions, Labor, and Individual Choice*, ed. David Wise, 193–215. Chicago: University of Chicago Press for NBER.

Johnson, Richard W. 1999. Distributional Implications of Social Security Reform for the Elderly: The Impact of Revising COLAs, the Normal Retirement Age, and the Taxation of Benefits. *National Tax Journal* 52 (September): 505–29.

Kahn, James A. 1988. Social Security, Liquidity, and Early Retirement. *Journal of Public Economics* 35, no. 1 (February): 97–117.

Kenkel, Donald S. 1991. Health Behavior, Health Knowledge, and Schooling. *Journal of Political Economy* 80:287–305.

Keppel, Kenneth G., Jeffrey N. Pearcy, and Diane K. Wagener. 2002. Trends in Racial and Ethnic-Specific Rates for the Health Status Indicators: United States, 1990–98. *Healthy People* no. 23. Centers for Disease Control, National Center for Health Statistics (January).

Kitagawa, E., and P. Hauser. 1973. *Differential Mortality in the United States: A Study in Socioeconomic Epidemiology*. Cambridge, Mass.: Harvard University Press.

Lantz, P. M., J. S. House, J. M. Lepkowski, D. R. Williams, R. P. Mero, and J. Chen. 1998. Socioeconomic Factors, Health Behaviors, and Mortality. *Journal of the American Medical Association* 279, no. 21 (June).

Leimer, Dean R. 1995. A Guide to Social Security Money's Worth Issues. *Social Security Bulletin* 58, no. 2 (Summer): 3–20.

Liebman, Jeffrey B. 2002. Redistribution in the Current U.S. Social Security System. In *The Distributional Aspects of Social Security and Social Security Reform*, ed. Martin Feldstein and Jeffrey B. Liebman, 11–48. Chicago: University of Chicago Press for NBER.

Lillard, L., and L. Waite. 1994. Till Death Do Us Part: Marital Disruption and Mortality. *American Journal of Sociology* 100, no. 5:1131–56.

REFERENCES

Loh, Eng Seng. 1996. Productivity Differences and the Marriage Wage Premium for White Males. *Journal of Human Resources* 31, no. 3:566–89.

Lumsdaine, Robin L., James A. Stock, and David A. Wise. 1995. Why Are Retirement Rates So High at Age 65? NBER working paper 5190. National Bureau of Economic Research, Cambridge, Mass. (July).

McGarry, Kathleen. 2002. Guaranteed Income: SSI and the Well-Being of the Elderly Poor. In *Distributional Aspects of Social Security and Social Security Reform*, 49–79. Chicago: University of Chicago Press for NBER.

Musgrave, R. A., and T. Thin. 1948. Income Tax Progression 1929–1948. *Journal of Political Economy* 56 (December): 498–514.

Pablos-Mendez, A. 1994. Mortality among Hispanics. *JAMA* 271:1237b.

Panis, Constantijn, and Lee Lillard. 1999. Near Term Model Development. Final report, contract no. 600-96-27335. RAND, Santa Monica, Calif.

Panis, Constantijn W. A., and Lee A. Lillard. 1996. Socioeconomic Differentials in the Return to Social Security. RAND report DRU-1327-NIA. RAND, Santa Monica, Calif. (February).

Preston, S. H., I. T. Elo, I. Rosenwaike, and M. Hill. 1996. African-American Mortality at Older Ages: Results of a Matching Study. *Demography* 33, no. 2 (May): 193–209.

Saffer, Henry, and Frank J. Chaloupka. 1999. Demographic Differences in the Demand for Alchohol and Illicit Drugs. In *The Economic Analysis of Substance Use and Abuse: An Integration of Econometric and Behavioral Economic Research*, ed. Frank J. Chaloupka et al., 187–211. Chicago and London: University of Chicago Press for NBER.,

Smith, Karen, Eric Toder, and Howard Iams. 2001. Lifetime Distributional Effects of Social Security Retirement Benefits. Prepared for the Third Annual Joint Conference for the Retirement Research Consortium, Making Hard Choices about Retirement, May 17–18, Washington, D.C.

Sorlie, P. D., E. Backlund, N. J. Johnson, and E. Rogot. 1993. Mortality by Hispanic Status in the United States. *JAMA* 270, no. 20:2464–68.

Sorlie, P., E. Rogot, R. Anderson, N. J. Johnson, and E. Backlund. 1992. Black-White Mortality Differences by Family Income. *Lancet* 340 (August): 346–50.

Stein, Herbert, and Murray Foss. 1999. *The Illustrated Guide to the American Economy*, 3rd ed. Washington, D.C.: AEI Press.

Steuerle, C. Eugene, and Jon M. Bakija. 1994. *Retooling Social Security for the 21st Century*. Washington, D.C.: Urban Institute Press.

Stock, James, and David Wise. 1990. Pensions, the Option Value of Work, and Retirement. *Econometrica* 58:1151–80.

Susin, Scott. 2002. Rent Vouchers and the Price of Low-Income Housing. *Journal of Public Economics* 83:109–52.

Tullock, Gordon. 1967. The Welfare Costs of Tariffs, Monopolies, and Theft. *Western Economic Journal* 5 (June): 224–32.

74 INCOME REDISTRIBUTION FROM SOCIAL SECURITY

Uccello, Cori E. 1998. Factors Influencing Retirement: Their Implications for Raising Retirement Age. American Association of Retired Persons Report #9810 (October).

U.S. Bureau of Economic Analysis. 2001. *Survey of Current Business* 81, no. 8. Washington, D.C.: U.S. Government Printing Office (August).

———. 2003. National Income and Product Accounts Tables. http://www.bea.doc.gov/bea/dn/nipaweb/index.asp (accessed December 3, 2003).

U.S. Census Bureau. 2001. *Money Income in the United States: 2000.* Washington, D.C.: U.S. Government Printing Office.

———. 2002a. Income 1999. http://www.census.gov/hhes/income/income99/99tablea.html (accessed January 9, 2002).

———. 2002b. http://www.census.gov/population/www/socdemo/hh-fam/p20-537_00.html (accessed January 4, 2002).

———. 2002c. *Statistical Abstract of the United States: 2001.* Washington, D.C.: U.S. Government Printing Office.

U.S. Centers for Disease Control. 2002a. National Center for Health Statistics: Fast Stats. http://www.cdc.gov/nchs/fastats (accessed January 9, 2002).

———. 2002b. National Center for Health Statistics: National Vital Statistics System. http://www.cdc.gov/nchs/nvss.htm (accessed January 8, 2002).

U.S. Social Security Administration. 2002a. Social Security Act Amendments of 1950: A Summary and Legislative History. http://www.ssa.gov/history/1950amend.html (accessed March 20, 2002).

———. 2002b. Automatic Increases. http://www.ssa.gov/OACT/COLA/CBB.html (accessed March 19, 2002).

———. 2002c. Fast Facts & Figures about Social Security, 2001. http://www.ssa.gov/statistics/fast_facts/2001/ff2001.pdf (accessed April 4, 2002).

———. 2002d. SSI Annual Statistical Report: Highlights 2000. http://www.ssa.gov/statistics/Supplement/2000/highlights.pdf (accessed April 15, 2002).

———. 2002e. Annual Statistical Supplement, 2000. http://www.ssa.gov/statistics/Supplement/2000/4b.pdf (accessed April 15, 2002).

———. 2003a. The 2002 OASDI Trustees Report. http://www.ssa.gov/OACT/TR/TR02/index.html (accessed November 20, 2003).

———. 2003b. Fast Facts & Figures about Social Security, 2002. http://www.ssa.gov/statistics/fast_facts/2002/ff2002.html (accessed October 23, 2003).

———. 2004 The 2004 OASDI Trustees Report. http://www.ssa.gov/OACT/TR/TR04/index.html (accessed September 29, 2004).

Welsh, Finis. 2001. Comment on Predictors of Mortality among the Elderly. In *Themes in the Economics of Aging*, ed. David Wise, 178. Chicago: University of Chicago Press for NBER.

About the Authors

Don Fullerton is the Addison Baker Duncan Centennial Professor of Economics at the University of Texas–Austin. Since finishing his PhD in economics at the University of California–Berkeley in 1978, he has taught at Princeton, the University of Virginia, and Carnegie Mellon University. From 1985 to 1987, he served as deputy assistant secretary of the U.S. Treasury for tax analysis.

Brent Mast is a statistician at the U.S. Department of Justice. His research focuses on education, crime, and public choice. He was research fellow at the Progress and Freedom Foundation, and research associate at the American Enterprise Institute, Florida Department of Corrections, and Florida State University. He has taught at Hobart and William Smith Colleges, John Jay College of Criminal Justice of the City University of New York, and Miami University of Ohio. He received his PhD in economics from Florida State University in 1996.

Board of Trustees

Bruce Kovner, *Chairman*
Chairman
Caxton Associates, LLC

Lee R. Raymond,
Vice Chairman
Chairman and CEO
Exxon Mobil Corporation

Tully M. Friedman, *Treasurer*
Chairman and CEO
Friedman Fleischer & Lowe LLC

Gordon M. Binder
Managing Director
Coastview Capital, LLC

Harlan Crow
Chairman and CEO
Crow Holdings

Christopher DeMuth
President
American Enterprise Institute

Morton H. Fleischer
Chairman and CEO
Spirit Finance Corporation

Christopher B. Galvin
Former Chairman and CEO
Motorola, Inc.

Raymond V. Gilmartin
Chairman, President, and CEO
Merck & Co., Inc.

Harvey Golub
Chairman and CEO, Retired
American Express Company

Robert F. Greenhill
Chairman and CEO
Greenhill & Co.

Roger Hertog
Vice Chairman
Alliance Capital Management Corporation

Martin M. Koffel
Chairman and CEO
URS Corporation

John A. Luke Jr.
Chairman and CEO
MeadWestvaco Corporation

L. Ben Lytle
Chairman Emeritus
Anthem, Inc.

Alex J. Mandl
CEO
Gemplus International SA

Robert A. Pritzker
President and CEO
Colson Associates, Inc.

J. Joe Ricketts
Chairman and Founder
Ameritrade Holding Corporation

Kevin B. Rollins
President and CEO
Dell Inc.

John W. Rowe
Chairman and CEO
Exelon Corporation

Edward B. Rust Jr.
Chairman and CEO
State Farm Insurance Companies

William S. Stavropoulos
Chairman
The Dow Chemical Company

Wilson H. Taylor
Chairman Emeritus
CIGNA Corporation

Marilyn Ware
Chairman Emerita
American Water

James Q. Wilson
Pepperdine University

Emeritus Trustees

Willard C. Butcher
Richard B. Madden
Robert H. Malott
Paul W. McCracken
Paul F. Oreffice
Henry Wendt

Officers

Christopher DeMuth
President

David Gerson
Executive Vice President

Jason Bertsch
Vice President, Marketing

Montgomery B. Brown
Vice President, Publications

The American Enterprise Institute for Public Policy Research

Founded in 1943, AEI is a nonpartisan, nonprofit research and educational organization based in Washington, D.C. The Institute sponsors research, conducts seminars and conferences, and publishes books and periodicals.

AEI's research is carried out under three major programs: Economic Policy Studies; Foreign Policy and Defense Studies; and Social and Political Studies. The resident scholars and fellows listed in these pages are part of a network that also includes ninety adjunct scholars at leading universities throughout the United States and in several foreign countries.

The views expressed in AEI publications are those of the authors and do not necessarily reflect the views of the staff, advisory panels, officers, or trustees.

Danielle Pletka
Vice President, Foreign and Defense Policy Studies

Council of Academic Advisers

James Q. Wilson, *Chairman*
Pepperdine University

Eliot A. Cohen
Professor and Director of Strategic Studies
School of Advanced International Studies
Johns Hopkins University

Gertrude Himmelfarb
Distinguished Professor of History Emeritus
City University of New York

Samuel P. Huntington
Albert J. Weatherhead III University Professor of Government
Harvard University

William M. Landes
Clifton R. Musser Professor of Law and Economics
University of Chicago Law School

Sam Peltzman
Ralph and Dorothy Keller Distinguished Service Professor of Economics
University of Chicago Graduate School of Business

Nelson W. Polsby
Heller Professor of Political Science
Institute of Government Studies
University of California–Berkeley

George L. Priest
John M. Olin Professor of Law and Economics
Yale Law School

Jeremy Rabkin
Professor of Government
Cornell University

Murray L. Weidenbaum
Mallinckrodt Distinguished
University Professor
Washington University

Richard J. Zeckhauser
Frank Plumpton Ramsey Professor
of Political Economy
Kennedy School of Government
Harvard University

Research Staff

Joseph Antos
Wilson H. Taylor Scholar in Health
Care and Retirement Policy

Leon Aron
Resident Scholar

Claude E. Barfield
Resident Scholar; Director, Science
and Technology Policy Studies

Roger Bate
Visiting Fellow

Walter Berns
Resident Scholar

Douglas J. Besharov
Joseph J. and Violet Jacobs
Scholar in Social Welfare Studies

Daniel Blumenthal
Resident Fellow

Karlyn H. Bowman
Resident Fellow

John E. Calfee
Resident Scholar

Charles W. Calomiris
Arthur F. Burns Scholar in
Economics

Veronique de Rugy
Research Fellow

Thomas Donnelly
Resident Fellow

Nicholas Eberstadt
Henry Wendt Scholar in Political
Economy

Eric M. Engen
Resident Scholar

Mark Falcoff
Resident Scholar Emeritus

Gerald R. Ford
Distinguished Fellow

John C. Fortier
Research Fellow

David Frum
Resident Fellow

Ted Gayer
Visiting Scholar

Reuel Marc Gerecht
Resident Fellow

Newt Gingrich
Senior Fellow

James K. Glassman
Resident Fellow

Jack Goldsmith
Visiting Scholar

Robert A. Goldwin
Resident Scholar

Scott Gottlieb
Resident Fellow

Michael S. Greve
John G. Searle Scholar

Robert W. Hahn
Resident Scholar; Director,
AEI-Brookings Joint Center
for Regulatory Studies

Kevin A. Hassett
Resident Scholar; Director,
Economic Policy Studies

Steven F. Hayward
F. K. Weyerhaeuser Fellow

Robert B. Helms
Resident Scholar; Director,
Health Policy Studies

Frederick M. Hess
Resident Scholar; Director,
Education Policy Studies

R. Glenn Hubbard
Visiting Scholar

Leon R. Kass
Hertog Fellow

Jeane J. Kirkpatrick
Senior Fellow

Herbert G. Klein
National Fellow

Marvin H. Kosters
Resident Scholar

Irving Kristol
Senior Fellow

Randall S. Kroszner
Visiting Scholar

Desmond Lachman
Resident Fellow

Michael A. Ledeen
Freedom Scholar

James R. Lilley
Senior Fellow

Lawrence B. Lindsey
Visiting Scholar

John R. Lott Jr.
Resident Scholar

John H. Makin
Visiting Scholar; Director,
Fiscal Policy Studies

Allan H. Meltzer
Visiting Scholar

Hedieh Mirahmadi
Visiting Scholar

Joshua Muravchik
Resident Scholar

Charles Murray
W. H. Brady Scholar

Michael Novak
George Frederick Jewett Scholar
in Religion, Philosophy, and Public
Policy; Director, Social and Political
Studies

Norman J. Ornstein
Resident Scholar

Richard Perle
Resident Fellow

Alex J. Pollock
Resident Fellow

Sarath Rajapatirana
Visiting Scholar

Michael Rubin
Resident Scholar

Sally Satel
Resident Scholar

Joel Schwartz
Visiting fellow

Daniel Shaviro
Visiting Scholar

J. Gregory Sidak
Resident Scholar

Radek Sikorski
Resident Fellow; Executive
Director, New Atlantic Initiative

Christina Hoff Sommers
Resident Scholar

Samuel Thernstrom
Managing Editor, AEI Press;
Director, W. H. Brady Program

Fred Thompson
Visiting Fellow

Peter J. Wallison
Resident Fellow

Scott Wallsten
Resident Scholar

Ben J. Wattenberg
Senior Fellow

John Yoo
Visiting Fellow

Karl Zinsmeister
J. B. Fuqua Fellow; Editor,
The American Enterprise